COURAGE

UNDER

FIRE

OVERCOMING THE ATTACKS OF SATAN
BY USING THE WORD OF GOD AND
THE BLOOD OF JESUS CHRIST.

"Behold, I give unto you power to tread on serpents and scorpions, and over all the power of the enemy: and nothing shall by any means hurt you." Luke 10:19

COURAGE UNDER FIRE!!

SHERON M. CLARKE

Copyright © 2013 SHERON M. CLARKE

ISBN 978-0-984 5428-2-6

All Scripture quotations are from the King James Version .

Request for information should be addressed to:

SHERON M. CLARKE

Tel. 301-642-8934

Email: clarke.sheron@yahoo.com

Contents

I. Acknowledgments

I first acknowledge my Lord and Savior Jesus Christ who implanted this book in my spirit and made it a reality. I thank God for my biological family and especially my father Mr. Cyprian Clarke for his unwavering love and support. I thank my Spiritual Leader, Pastor Dorothy Lartey and the members of Power of the Highest International Ministries.

I am overjoyed to be connected to the anointed Intercessors of Ministry Without Walls International, Inc who are truly the wind beneath my wings. I thank God for sisters Monica Miller and Sheila McNabb who have been praying for years and waiting for this manifestation. I am also grateful to sister Joan McKenzie Bellille who prays with me every Sunday morning before we go out on the battlefield. Ministry Without Walls Intercessors you are all a God sent.

COURAGE UNDER FIRE!!

THE CHANGE

Seek and you shall find
So my thirsty soul wandered and sought for over a decade
Years of wasted emotions, good deeds, kind thoughts
Were all in vain because I still had not found
Persistence and gentle guidance of the Almighty
Fueled my weary soul and directed me to the door of my
salvation

Happiness took over
My soul jumped for joy when the Holy Spirit took control
of my life
I yearn for perfection in His sight
I yearn to please Him in every move that I make
A day is nought without triumphant praises and thanks to
the Most High

Most mortals will not understand the change
Friends might be confused; even envious
It's not easy; but its even worse for them – consciences
have been disturbed
But that won't stop me
I'm on the King's agenda, you see.

Sheron M. Clarke
February 8, 1994

5

II. Preface

God does not call the equipped, He equips the called and what an assurance that is for someone like me who is totally dependent on His guidance.   Over fifteen years ago when the Lord showed me in a dream the title of this book I initially thought that it was someone else's book that He wanted me to read.   When it dawned on me that I was chosen as the one to write such a book I was truly humbled.

When God places a dream in your spirit nothing can replace that dream. The dream will become dormant for a while because of the trials and the testing that you have to go through. However, every now and then when you need encouragement to go the next mile He will remind you of where He wants to take you. Some of you have to take detour to get to the ultimate prize that God has for you but that does not mean you will never reach it. Keep pressing toward your goal. In my life there were two, three or four wars going on at the same time but what was happening was that my story was being written so that I could encourage others.

While your story is being written it might not seem like a big deal to some and it might even seem to others as if you have lost your mind. Some will even dare to whisper behind your back, call you names and dare to call you worthless. However, in I Timothy 6:12 Paul was encouraging Timothy to fight the good fight of faith, lay hold on eternal life, whereunto thou art also called, and has professed a good profession before many witnesses. We will get weary in any war but we cannot give up in the midst of battle. Know that if the Enemy is fighting you it is worth fighting back because he has seen your blessing and he is trying to rob you. Not only must you not give up for your own sake but there are also some folks who are watching you and they are admiring your grit and tenacity. Know that you will be a source of strength to them because they have seen you maneuver your way through spiritual land mines, spiritual booby traps, "friendly" fire from every direction and yet emerged wiser, stronger, more loving and more compassionate.

This is why it is of utmost importance that we move in the timing of God. This book could not have been written ten or even five years ago but it is for this time - now. It is amazing how God allowed me to know my timing by sending certain people who need to be encouraged most by this book to be coming up to me for prayers. Some have never heard the term spiritual warfare before yet they were in the fight of their lives and they were not equipped.

III. Introduction

There are many devices in a man's heart; nevertheless the counsel of the LORD, that shall stand Proverbs 19:21. This is a book for the people whose lives took a different turn from what they had envisioned it to be – that is almost everyone.

There were plans, goals and dreams that you put a time frame on. You say to yourself that by the time you are, twenty-five or by the time you are thirty or by the time you are forty you are certain that these dreams and aspirations would have materialized already.

Well, that was what I said to myself. Life seemed to be going in a positive direction. Everything I put my hands to seemed to prosper and so as a young person the goals, accomplishments and dreams seemed all within my reach. I felt as if there was absolutely nothing that I could not achieve with hard work, proper planning and every ounce of determination. Life was manageable and I knew that the best was yet to come. I truly believed that it was not only coming but within the time frame that I had outlined in my head and on my little notepad.

After acquiring all the education I needed marriage and children would be the next step by age thirty and by age forty I would be financially secure, stable and solid as a rock. The only problem with this plan was that I did not include the real Rock. That Rock I am talking about is Jesus Christ. I knew He was there but God to me at that time was in the background and when I really needed Him then I would call on Him. After all, how was this going to be accomplished if I did not take charge? I was very sociable, likable and reliable. I knew a lot of people in high position. I was also well trained and very good at my job, this gave me favor and as a result of which the doors were wide open – the sky was the limit.

I should have known, however, that God had another plan for my life based on the fact that people would literally pick me out of the crowd to ask me if I was a Christian. This would often irritate me because at that particular time I was not thinking church. Let me say that it was just not in the forefront of my mind. However, the Holy Spirit has a way of subtly drawing us unto Him without us even realizing it.

The offices were located in a new building, the company was newly formed by our then Prime Minister. The décor was beautiful, the staff was so happy and loving, and the morale was really high in the workplace. However, on the way to this beautiful edifice you were liable to see anything and what would greatly disturb me was to see the homeless or the mentally deranged eating out of the garbage. It would bring tears to my eyes and my heart would be so broken over their condition.

If you have ever wondered how you could help make this world a better place then this book is for you. If you have ever thought that the Enemy would never try to derail your plans, then this book is definitely for you. If you have ever doubted the cunningness of the Enemy to sabotage the purpose of God for your life, then this book is truly for you.

We can have all the plans in the world but it is God's purpose that will prevail. When you are marked by God for a specific task you can run but you cannot hide as the saying goes. Even if He, God, has to use the Enemy to bring forth the manifestation of His will into your life.

"IF YOU LIVE YOUR YESTERDAYS TODAY YOU WILL NEVER ENJOY YOUR TOMORROWS."

Sheron M. Clarke

CHAPTER ONE

THE DREAM

Now the Lord had said to Abram, get thee out of thy country,
and from thy kindred, and from thy father's house unto a land
that I will shew thee: Genesis 12:1

While living in Jamaica one Saturday I was taking my
evening nap and I had a dream. I dreamt that I was in the United
States of America and I was working as a maid. When I woke
up I told the dream to my girlfriend whose nickname is Gut. I
remember her saying "If you want to go to America to work as a
maid that is your business!" In other words, she was mad. "A
maid?" Based on my lifestyle she just could not understand why
I would even get such a dream. It just did not make sense to
either of us. At that time I was a backslider and she was not a
Christian so we never gave it much thought.

By the time I had this dream I had managed to put myself
through college and was in a job that offered me a fairly
comfortable lifestyle. This included full health benefits, pension
plan, lots of perks and the prospect of growth within the
company. So when I had this dream I had no intention of
traveling to the United States except to go shop and return home
as I had done in the past.

In Isaiah 55:8 it states for my thoughts are not your thoughts,
neither are your ways my ways, saith the Lord. Needless to say,
a few months later I landed at the Philadelphia Airport on my
way to New Jersey to stay with a cousin whom I met only once
or twice before. The major reason for this change of plan was
that I had a brother who was a senior at Howard University on a
partial scholarship. He was in his final year and it was very
financially challenging for him. He was doing his best to make

it and so as the eldest of six children I had this urge and felt this responsibility to do more financially for him. Not only was I going to help him and ultimately the family but I also thought it was a wonderful opportunity to kill two birds with one stone. I also wanted to get away from a broken relationship. However, I found out the hard way that pain will tag along uninvited no matter how far you may go. Not only is the pain in your soul a constant reminder of a fragmented heart but your vision also becomes relationally blurred.

Shortly after being in New Jersey a former coworker, Agnes, who had migrated to Florida encouraged me to come and stay with her. The plan was so that I could work in the job that she was about to leave. She worked very hard at convincing me that Ft. Lauderdale had much more prospects as opposed to living in South Jersey.

I told my cousin my plans, packed my bags and headed for Florida. When I got there eager to begin working, my friend told me that the job she had for me she had an argument with her employer and told her off. In other words, that was the end of that job. So I decided to roll up my sleeves so to speak and make the best of the situation. I also noticed that she was not in a rush to look for another job.

Thankfully, God opened another door and so once when I was not able to collect my check she went and collected it for me. Yes she did, she even cashed it and used the money to pay her phone bill; at that time I had incurred no phone bill. When I asked her about my check and also why she was not working her explanation was that she needed to pay her phone bill and also she was tired so she was now taking a break. It dawned on me, of course, that she was really not a true friend. She had an ulterior motive for my being there and it was a diabolical plot that included her younger sister who was about my age.

13

COURAGE UNDER FIRE!!

One weekend another friend of mine who lived in New York visited us in Ft. Lauderdale. She did not particularly care for my Ft. Lauderdale friend and so she suggested that I relocated to New York. I had known her for many years prior to coming to the United States and we had a great relationship. She shared with me that she was about to leave her job for a better one and so she would look for a two- bedroom apartment in New York for us. She asked me to please think about it.

Even though I did not have a close relationship with the Lord, at that time, I thank God for favor. I worked seven days/nights per week saving as much as I could in order to relocate to New York. One afternoon as I was entering one of the elevators in the building that I was working in I ran into a childhood friend of mine who happened to be entering the next elevator. The last time we had seen each other we were children. She called out from the elevator "I know those eyes." I recognized her voice and immediately responded "I know those eyes too." The wonderful thing about this was that our facial features had not changed much.

Her name is Lilly White and I still believe her eyes are bigger than mine. It has been an ongoing joke between us. It so happens that she lived in Miami and worked in the same building that I was also in. We had such a connection. It was so refreshing to meet someone with a good heart. People seeing us together could never believe that we were apart for so long and yet had such a wonderful relationship. She reminded me how to laugh again. We really enjoyed each other to the point where she was so disappointed when I informed her that I was in the process of relocating to New York. There was, however, such an urge in my spirit that I knew that as much as I would have loved to stay in Miami I had to go.

COURAGE UNDER FIRE!!

I called Agnes and told her that my intentions were to go back up north. So I eventually went and got my belongings from her apartment with the intention of taking up my friend's offer to relocate to New York instead of South Jersey. I worked for a few more months in Miami Beach and I really enjoyed the people, the area and my friend Lilly and her family.

When I got to New York my friend looked the same on the outside but her inside was cold. She obviously had a change of mind but forgot to share it with me. There was no discussion, no argument but most of us can pretty much tell when we are not welcome. My only conclusion was that she asked me to share with her when she thought she needed help. However, after everything was settled, she realized that she could manage so her plans no longer included me. It knocked the wind out of me for a brief moment but I thank God that even though I was not walking as close to Him as I ought to, I do bounce back very quickly from disappointments. My stay in New York was very brief and so feeling a twinge of embarrassment, to say the least, I made my way back to New Jersey.

One day as I was going through my suitcase that had been at Agnes' apartment I realized that an envelop with important documents were missing. I truly believe that Agnes took it based on her character and her insistence that I relocated to Florida. For her to have done this to another human being that she called friend was just unthinkable to me. I had only known her as a coworker so I never had a very close relationship with her. However, I never imagined she could have been so mean spirited to me.

I had to take a long hard look at the way our paths had crossed. The first year that we worked together back home the company doubled my salary based on my efficiency and productivity. It sounds hard to believe but true. The following

15

year because of my work ethics I still got a decent salary increase. I was the "kid" so to speak in the corporation but my work ethics did not go unnoticed. I believe in excellence and loyalty and I was very good at what I did so within two years I was working as the Executive Assistant to the Vice President of the company. We have a saying in my country that states "Every skin teeth is a not a laugh." Translation – every grin is not true laughter.

In I Samuel 16 the Lord sent Samuel, the Prophet, to the house of Jesse to anoint one of his sons as king. In the beginning God did not tell Samuel which one of the sons was to be anointed. So Samuel did not know which one he just followed God's instruction by getting the oil and going to Jesse's house. This is a spiritual principle many Christians need to learn. When God speaks we need to move accordingly. God is not obligated to explain every detail of His plan beforehand. Sometimes He may choose to do that but most times He does not. When Samuel went to the house of Jesse he called his sons from the oldest, Eliab, down to the seventh son. Samuel was so sure that Eliab would be the one because he so looked like a potential king. His physical structure was so impressive. In verse 7 of the same chapter God told Samuel not to look on his countenance, or on his height because He has refused him. God told Samuel that He sees not like man for man looks on the outward appearance but He, God, looks on the heart.

Going back to New Jersey was no easy task for me. I remember going over everything in my mind and thinking that there were no disagreements. Even when Agnes collected my paycheck we did not quarrel, I simply let it go. I really started questioning the wickedness of the human heart but could not find the answer. In Jeremiah 17:9 it says that the heart is deceitful above all things, and desperately wicked: who can know it?

A few months later I was standing at a sink in Connecticut washing my new employer's dishes and the tears began to flow. Nothing was working as planned. Thus the dream became a reality. The comfort and stability I had known in my country, I no longer had. I never thought of myself as sheltered but I definitely was. I was encountering negativity such as envy, jealousy, and deceit among other evils on a magnitude like I had never experienced before coming to the United States. It felt as if I had just entered the university called "Life" and I was not enjoying it.

For one and a half year I moved from New Jersey to Florida, to New York and back to New Jersey trying to find peace and stability. Of course, life got worse because one cannot find peace and stability outside of God. It is even worse if God has a call upon your life and that is the farthest thing on your mind. During this time I was robbed, deceived and obviously a threat to my fellow countrywomen who were here before me. There seems to be an unspoken fear that some folks who have been in the States before you have and it is that you might surpass them. As a result of which sometimes there is an underlying jealousy that can lead to sabotage when the heart is not right.

The reason why I appreciate and love the Lord so much is that He keeps us even when we are not thinking about Him. He watches over us when we are so consumed with people, our stuff and everything that is not a Kingdom issue.

God in His grace and mercy opened another door for me to take care of a beautiful eight- week old baby girl. Her name is Elizabeth. I loved her as if she was my own child. The family was really wonderful and still is even to this day. I started feeling like I was finally finding my bearings in the United States for the first time. Job-wise I was feeling more settled but my thoughts were always on improving myself and striving to enjoy the standard of living that I was accustomed to. I knew, however, that I was where I needed to be at that particular time and so I made the best of it.

I would commute to work from south New Jersey on a weekly basis to upstate New York. One Sunday night I was not feeling well and I asked God to please let me make it to the weekend so I could see my doctor. That was not to be because the next morning I had to be taken to the emergency room because I was having a miscarriage.

Attending church was still not a part of my schedule at that time. I was living by the world's standard but in times of trouble it is amazing how we instinctively know to call upon God. As human beings at some point in our lives we will get to that place where we are faced with such helplessness that we have no alternative but to call upon a higher power. Some call Him Energy, some call Him Force among other names and yes He is all that and much more. However, I choose to call Him, Jehovah because that is His name. He is the true and living God. He created us with a void in our hearts for Him and nothing or no one else can fill that vacuum. We tend to serve ourselves and everyone else and when we get to the end of our rope, thankfully some of us will look up to Him for help. God's desire is, however, for Him to be our first not our last resort.

As I lay on that brown and cream checkered couch in my employer's den that morning the only pain I felt was the pain of shame. At this very moment, subconsciously I placed a very high and thick wall around my heart with an attached sign saying, "I will protect me at all cost."

I thank God that there are still some good, kindhearted people in this world. My employer's mother, Mrs. Fioretti who is such a sweet person came to the house to take care of me during this difficult time. I can see her in my minds eye just as if it was yesterday. She was holding on to the banister coming upstairs with a bowl of soup to give me so that I could rest. We laughed and talked just having a wonderful time. I will never forget her as long as I live. God has a way of encouraging us not to lose hope in humanity or even in ourselves when we have been given the hand of adversity. This family unknowingly, gave me hope to keep walking out of disappointments because in my heart I felt as if they cared.

Three years later the family had their second little girl and her name is Charlotte. Different personality, I could tell this one was a fighter. She was very quick, she kept me going and when Charlotte was old enough it was a joy having them both. No experience in our life is ever wasted if we have the proper perspective. I felt the urge to move on when Charlotte was one year old. The family kept expanding and a few years afterwards came Isabel whom I affectionately call "Isabeli".

I believe every single experience is a part of the missing piece of life's major puzzle that God is putting together. It is preparation for your future. The Lord said in Jeremiah 29:11 "For I know the thoughts that I think toward you, saith the Lord, thoughts of peace, and not of evil, to give you an expected end." For us to walk in this kind of prosperity and to receive the good end that God has for us we have to be totally reprogrammed and rewired from doing our own thing.

Every test and every challenge is designed to draw us closer to God. I believe that some of us are farther from God than others and so we have to go through more difficulties. I then made a conscious decision to look forward and stop crying over life as I had known it in my country.

"WORSHIP IS A WORTHY PATH"

Sheron M. Clarke

CHAPTER TWO

DESTINY WRAPPED IN DISASTER

And we know that all things work together for good to them that love God, to them who are called according to His purpose. Romans 8:28

An acquaintance of mine told me about a friend of hers who was looking for a roommate. She described her as a wonderful older woman who attends church regularly. She tried to assure me that we would both get along very well because back in the island she had always admired me quietly sitting on my porch reading. She went on to say that this arrangement would work because this woman is not only very quiet but she also attends church.

I thought to myself and said well if this lady goes to church then she should not be that bad. I was leery about this based on my past experiences but my consolation was that she might be different based on the fact that she goes to church. I then decided to relocate to Brooklyn, New York instead of commuting to South Jersey every weekend.

I believe that the reason why I had no peace in my life was because I was a prodigal who God was calling for a specific purpose but I needed a lot of preparation. At this particular time, however, I was now at the place where I was looking for a church, at least in my mind. Which meant that I was getting closer to the will of God but still not quite there. The reality is that so many people will keep saying that they are looking for a church but they are not actively searching. It has crossed their mind once or twice to find a church but they have not taken any action. In their mind, however, they really believe they are looking. It is only an intention.

COURAGE UNDER FIRE!!

At the age of 16, I had given my life to Jesus Christ at a Billy Graham Evangelistic Crusade in Montego Bay, Jamaica. One year later my love for the Lord was so deep that I stood at the back of my house and made an oath. I said "Lord I want to always have this wonderful feeling that I am now experiencing with you. So God if I should ever backslide and you are calling me and calling me and I will not turn around before I get to the place of no return God please kill me." I said it at age 17 and I meant it.

The problem with this vow was that a few years later I had forgotten that I had said it to God. Even when I was going through the various betrayals, deceptions, living in sin and challenges I kept trying to fix things on my own. When you have wandered far from God and the things of God your mind become very polluted by the world. The Spiritual light of Christ will be diminished and the darkness of this world will come and put its graffiti on the wall of your soul. Spiritual purity goes to the backseat because the world has no godly standard and now you have blended in. The desire of God is no longer a priority. As a matter of fact, He has become an afterthought until you are facing danger.

If you have ever given your life to the Lord Jesus Christ, your spirit has been regenerated which means it is no longer dead to the things of God. The flesh and the spirit are enemies and so that is why there will always be constant conflict within you especially when you have backslidden. I will say, however, that this conflict will only be for a time if you do not surrender because after a while your heart will become very hard and callous to the Spirit of God. The longer you stay away from God is the less shame, the less guilt and the less remorse you will have over your sin. Your spirit becomes malnourished and your flesh is well fed.

COURAGE UNDER FIRE!!

Shortly after the conversation with my acquaintance I was introduced to my future roommate, Miss Williams. She seemed very quiet and reserved, did not say much at all. Now that I look back I realize that she was not merely observing but she was trying to discern the imprints of my soul. That same night I met her I had a dream. All I can remember in this dream was that there was so much blood that after all these years it still makes me extremely sick to my stomach just thinking about it.

The next week Miss Williams and I met at the apartment again to go over the final details before moving in. There was just something about her demeanor that I could not quite put my finger on so I asked her if she still wanted us to share space. She said "um um."

Now, after all the negative experiences I have had with friends one would think that this would send me running in the opposite direction. What I have discovered is that at the core of my being I genuinely love the human soul but God had to train me to be more discerning. I have this heart of always wanting to trust people. I never believe that I should use my previous experience to blacklist every future acquaintance. In addition to that I had never lived by myself. I am from a large family and even when I was on campus at college my side of the room was full with friends. Any friend who needed a place to stay or needed to stay on campus to finish their assignment would always have a place to sleep. It never occurred to me not to share food or space even with those whose families had more resources than mine. Growing up our family never had much financial resources but being selfish was not a part of our upbringing. My parents were not in church every Sunday but there was this belief that God would always provide and He faithfully did. It was such a part of my being to always have folks around me that even after my experiences I was about to sign a lease with a total stranger.

COURAGE UNDER FIRE!!

Very shortly after we moved into the apartment she invited me to church for Easter Sunday service. I was so excited that I went out immediately and got a church outfit. When I got to church I loved the songs, I loved the preaching and I could hardly believe that I was finally in church. My spirit was so hungry for the word and I was like a sponge absorbing everything. Miss Williams did not have to invite me twice because I was in church every Sunday and also at the mid week service. This was when I wondered what on earth kept me from the house of God for so long. I was a prodigal returning home and it felt great.

Friday night service was dedicated to the youth but all age group would be present. I would participate on Friday nights by reading one of the poems that I had written. I was really having fun in the church and the Pastor saw the excitement that I had for the things of God and so he encouraged it. I was growing in leaps and bounds in the spirit and I loved every moment of it. In Psalm 63: 1-3 David cried out to the Lord and said "O God, thou art my God; early will I seek thee: my soul thirsteth for thee, my flesh longeth for thee in a dry and thirsty land, where no water is; To see thy power and thy glory, so as I have seen thee in the sanctuary. Because thy lovingkindness is better than life, my lips shall praise thee." For us to grow spiritually we need to be hungry for God.

If you are a Christian and you are spiritually bored the problem is not with God it is with you. Your soul needs to be watered with the word of God. You need to jump start your prayer life by crying out to God for cleansing and a fresh infilling of the Holy Spirit. You need to remove all the dead weight that is hindering you so you can enter that place of true worship. There can be no façade or gimmick, God just wants us to be real before Him. We can hide our true feelings from friends and family but we cannot hide from God, so why do we

24

pretend? All we do is block our blessings. Jesus says in John 4: 23 "But the hour cometh, and now is, when the true worshippers shall worship the Father in spirit and in truth: for the father seeketh such to worship him."

You cannot be a true worshipper and be bored in your relationship with Jesus Christ or be stagnant. Anything that is stagnant is on the verge of dying or is already dead. We serve the true and living God and there is nothing stagnant about Him. He is the type of God who wants to have sweet fellowship with His people. He came down in the cool of the day in the Garden of Eden to commune with Adam. He created us for His purpose and for His pleasure. God must be worshipped by any means necessary because He is God. He says if we do not praise Him then the very rocks will cry out, so no matter what He must be praised. I declare that no rock is going to cry out in my place.

When you have tapped into the realm of being a true worshipper you are a threat to the Devil. He is first of all reminded of the fact that he no longer has that privilege. He lost his job because he wanted to be number one and God was not having that. There can only be one God and so Lucifer was kicked out of heaven along with one third of the angels, his followers. Low and behold here come these beings formed from mere dust, getting all this attention from the King of kings and the Lord of lords. God's love baffles me as well as David because he said in Psalm 8:4-5 "What is man, that thou art mindful of him? And the son of man, that thou visitest him: For thou hast made him a little lower than the angels, and hast crowned him with glory and honor. Thou madest him to have dominion over the works of thy hands; thou has put all things under his feet." This, of course, is the reason why Satan is so jealous of us. He knows that when we worship our God in spirit and in truth that is where we get our breakthrough. He knows that when we are in worship he cannot come into that realm with us. So he tries his very best to get us to be lazy in our worship and to be so fleshly that we cannot really enjoy the beauty of true worship. When we worship our God, Satan gets a headache because when he thinks about the beauty of heaven, the position that he had and the way he messed up his future he gets even more tormented.

That is why he will do anything and everything to try and stop it. But my Bible says in I John 4:4 "Ye are of God, little children and have overcome them: because greater is He that is in you than he that is in the world." My brothers and sisters worship is a worthy path. These were the words God spoke into my spirit a year ago.

Every Sunday Miss Williams and I would go to church together and one day in church the Pastor mistakenly called her Miss Williams instead of calling her by her real name. She got very furious with me. She turned to me and asked me how could Pastor not know her name after she had been there for seven years yet he knew my name and I just came. At that time I did not think much about her comments or her attitude toward me until much later on. I wanted to believe that everyone was really nice and the ones who weren't were just having a bad day. However, in this case Miss Williams was not just having a bad day she had the spirit of anger, jealousy and envy controlling her. I chose not to pay it much attention at that time.

Many Friday nights after coming home from youth service she would say to me that I was coming home with my friends again. I asked her what was she talking about but then she would not say anything else. One night after her statement I got angry with God because I was asking Him who could be following me in the spirit. I started talking to God about this and saying that I was living right as far as I know so what is this and what could this mean. I had no one to share this with and Miss Williams had no explanation she would only make statements. Whether she was seeing something or not her intentions were not good. I realized afterwards that Miss Williams was trying to instill fear in my heart.

The Enemy has a divide and conquer mentality. If he can get us to be living in fear then that would cause us to be spiritually and mentally fragmented. In other words, it will break our fellowship with God. Fear and faith cannot dwell in the same space one has to be the more dominant emotion. Fear is such a negative emotion that it will always try to overpower the faith that is in us as long as we are alive. I John 4:18 says "There is no fear in love; but perfect love casteth out fear: because fear hath torment. He that feareth is not made perfect in love."

That is why it is so important that as Christians we feed our spirit daily. Let the word of God permeate your soul. When this is the case you will even dream the word of God because it has become so much a part of your subconscious. This will not allow fear to come in and take up residence in your spirit, soul or body. Fear is torment and that is of the devil. If Satan can get us to be fearful then what will happen is that it will open a door for him and his imps to enter into our lives. In other words, we have given Satan legal access into our lives. He cannot enter unless we open the door for him or God gives him permission.

One of the ways we open the door is by having sin in our lives. He will use any means necessary to get us to open the door. He will use temptation, doubt, fear, lie, he doesn't care as long as he has an opening. Only then can he come in our lives and cause disasters like sicknesses, diseases, accidents, family breakups, addictions and the list goes on.

The Bible said For God hath not given us the spirit of fear; but of power, and of love, and of a sound mind in II Timothy

1:7. Fear is one of the many weapons that Satan has in his arsenal to try to defeat the children of God. If we are living in fear of him or what he can do to us then what we are saying is that we do not trust our God. We are also saying that our God is not able to take care of us. What a travesty? Our God is All Powerful and All Mighty. He is Almighty God and as His children we have also inherited some power. Jesus said in Luke 10:19 "I have given you power over every power of the enemy to trample serpents and scorpions in the name of Jesus."

God directed me right where He wanted me. I was at the place spiritually and physically where I was ready to learn of Him. Now God was about to mold me and fashion me for His purpose. All things work together for good to them that love God and are called according to his purpose as stated in Romans 8:28. It was in God's divine purpose that Miss Williams and I met. Regardless of what others did to me God's hand was in this all the way. Know my brothers and sisters that when the Enemy comes in like a flood God will lift up a standard against him according to Isaiah 59:19.

So many incidents were going on around me but because I was not experienced in spiritual battles and was a baby in the spirit I just thought it was a part of life. Looking back now I shudder to think that I never realized what was going on and with whom I was sharing. So many people are living in that state of spiritual oblivion right at this moment. Some refuse to believe like I did that someone who does not know them, someone whom they had no quarrel with, someone whom they probably looked up to as a mother figure or someone whom they admire as a role model could be so evil.

One day I was home and she came in from shopping and she held a black underwear in the palm of her right hand. It was not in a bag it was opened up in her right hand and she said "I bought this for you." I said "For me?" She answered "Yes". I thought it so strange because I wondered why would she want to buy underwear for me. I did not need any underwear and I was wondering why wasn't it in a bag. I really did not want it but a part of me did not want to offend her since she was older than I was. I said "Ok." I took it, washed it and wore, and washed it and wore it multiple times thinking nothing more of it.

One year after living in this apartment we moved to a bigger place. By this time, I was at a different stage in my spiritual journey with the Lord and my spiritual senses were much sharper but I still had a lot to learn. I knew something was wrong but witchcraft was the farthest thing on my mind. I had been asking God to sharpen the spirit of discernment so that I could spot mine enemies a mile away. God has such a sense of humor because little did I know how much He was giving me my desire. The "joke" was that there was a deadly enemy right under my nose and I could not even smell it.

We moved to a nicer place in a better neighborhood but there was one thing that struck me about this new place. It was dark. The bathroom was dark. The living room that led into the kitchen had one window so the kitchen was also dark. This was the only thing that bothered me about renting this apartment. Miss Williams liked it and out of respect for her I submitted once again. It was a split-level apartment and the bedrooms had sunlight coming through the windows so I thought maybe I could live with this, at least for a while.

What I observed was that Miss Williams had no desire of consecrating the place to the Lord even though she kept telling me that she was in church all her life. We moved in without prayer. I later went through the house with my Bible in hand and blessed the house including her bedroom. Yes I was getting bolder in the spirit.

COURAGE UNDER FIRE!!

By this my spiritual eyes were getting a bit sharper because I had more of the word of God in me. I really tried to love the new home but it was too dark and had an eerie feeling and a spirit of heaviness. I knew that we were not alone in this apartment. I would also see shadows here and there moving throughout the place. I believe that she was seeing them also but by this the relationship was of such that she would get very abrupt when responding to me.

One night I was sitting on my bed watching a Bishop T.D. Jakes video when I saw a dark shadow passed by my door. I could tell that it was a male in its thirties or mid forties. It looked at me while passing but kept walking toward the bathroom that was adjoining my bedroom. I sat still on my bed and kept looking toward my bedroom door. Within a few seconds it emerged from the bathroom and with its back pressing against my bedroom wall it was walking sideways slowly coming toward where I was sitting on my bed. I rebuked it in the Name of Jesus and ordered it to get out. I must have scared the people in the neighborhood because I could see lights in nearby homes coming on with great urgency.

The Lord is my light and my salvation whom shall I fear. He is the strength of my life of whom shall I be afraid Psalm 27: 1. The more we read the word of God is the stronger our prayer lives will become. We should also get in the habit of charging our atmosphere and we do so by at times reading the scriptures aloud. The basis for a strong prayer life is to know and repeat God's word back to Him. His word is also His will and He cannot deny His word if we ask with the right motive. As we build a strong prayer life then our courage will also increase.

God led me to be working for an agency that placed me at a bank while building my cosmetics business part time. As a result of which I did not have time to waste with Miss Williams' increasingly bad attitude plus I was enjoying church. I was focused on building the life that I had envisioned even before I came to this country. The ambition was still there in spite of the setbacks I had experienced.

Now that I was a Believer in Christ and I had learned that everything else is subject to fail and is temporary, I decided that my only trust was going to be in my Lord and Savior Jesus Christ. I had finally surrendered to God and He was teaching me how to love Him and to love myself. I was in the relationship of my life and I was very grateful to Miss Williams for inviting me to church. Paul said in Philippians 4:4 "Rejoice in the Lord always and again I say rejoice." I give God thanks for my enemies. When we are in the midst of the challenge it is hard to give thanks. However, if we can get to that place where we can thank Him while we are going through then we would have matured spiritually. If you want to baffle Satan and to have him scratch his head then worship God while you are still in the fire. We should let Satan also scratch his head in wonderment when he is waiting for us to throw in the towel and call it quits.

It seems as if Miss Williams was hoping that I was either going to be as evil as she was or another pew warmer that would be ineffective in the Kingdom of God. Apparently the Enemy's plans backfired in his face because when Miss Williams saw that I was growing and on fire for the Lord she became angrier and angrier as the days went by. She was not a happy camper.

My Pastor, at the time, had encouraged the congregation to get into the habit of fasting. He believed that every Christian should learn the discipline of fasting, even for half a day. So I got in the habit of fasting every Wednesday for half a day. I thank God that I always obeyed those who were put in charge over me. I started conditioning my mind to at least try and see what would happen if I skipped a meal. Behold, to obey is better

31

than sacrifice and to hearken than the fat of rams I Samuel 15:22. If you want to tap into the anointing you must be obedient to especially those who are your spiritual leaders and learn to be submissive. God is looking for a heart that is teachable and humble which is a prerequisite for greater anointing.

I truly believe that fasting is the added fuel that a Christian needs in his or her prayer life to give it that added power. In Matthew 17 the Bible relates the story of a father who came to Jesus' disciples asking them to cast out the demons that were terrorizing his son. The demons would often cast the boy in the fire and in the water trying to kill him. The disciples were unable to command the demons to leave. When Jesus came and rebuked the demons to come out, the disciples asked him privately how come they were not able to do it. Jesus replied in verse 21 by saying "Howbeit this kind goeth not out but by prayer and fasting." Fasting is a spiritual discipline that Christians need to adapt from our Lord. People from other faiths religiously fast to their gods. How much more should we who have a relationship with the True and Living God learn the discipline of fasting as demonstrated by Jesus Christ?

There are some evil spirits that will not budge when we pray simply because they are not impressed with our mediocre prayer lives. They can tell how strong we are and how much fire is in us based on the brightness of the light that radiates from us. Jesus Christ of Nazareth is that light Who lives in us but if there is more junk than Christ we cannot fool the demons. Demons know the difference. They are definitely not all knowing as our God but they can tell when we confront them if we are hypocrites or not. They are able to tell if we have a relationship with the Lord or if we are just pew warmers. Nothing is wrong with going to church, you ought to go but there is a difference when you have an intimate relationship with Jesus Christ. In Acts 19 the demons said to the seven sons of Sceva, Jesus I know, Paul I know but who are you? What a beaten those seven men got? The Bible said that they fled out of that house naked and wounded. Fasting is the catalyst that lubricates and energizes our prayer life. There is something about denying flesh and beating it into subjection that allows our spirit to soar in the Lord.

Remember the Lord says that no flesh shall glory in His presence. When we approach the throne of grace daily, if it is a fleshly approach our spiritual growth will be haphazard, sporadic or not at all. We never know what our next challenge in life is going to be and so it is best that we live a consecrated lifestyle unto our Lord. The reason being that there will come a time when trouble, sickness or disaster will come up on you and if you do not have a strong prayer life you will lose faith at the first sign of an overcast.

The spiritually mature is not immune from challenges that will come into their lives and sometimes very suddenly. Sometimes you never saw it coming, it caught you unaware and you are stunned. We are still living on earth and that is why it is so important that prayer and worship also become an integral part of our daily lives. Even when this is the case, there are times when all we can do is groan because of the warfare. Romans 8: 26 says "Likewise the Spirit also helpeth our infirmities: for we know not what we should pray for as we ought: but the Spirit itself maketh intercession for us with groanings which cannot be uttered." Sometimes when the situation in our lives seems unbearable all we can do is to groan and say "Jesus, Jesus, Jesus." He also said in His word that He would never give us more than we can bear I Corinthians 10:13.

I was in deep sleep one night when I dreamt that a tall, black man dressed in full white robe and white headdress stood before me. I held back my head to look up in his face then asked him "Why is it there is so much good in the world and people still find the bad things to do?" He did not answer me. He dipped his right index finger in oil that he had in his left hand and made the sign of the cross on my forehead. When he made the cross on my forehead some of the oil fell on my tongue. I staggered off the bed drunk in the spirit but half awake. I stumbled into the bathroom where the Lord purged my body as I sat for a good while on the commode.

The next morning I told Miss Williams about my dream and what happened to me afterwards. Her only words were "You must be careful who you eat from." I knew that I did not eat anything from anyone because I had been taught from a young age by my father to be very careful about eating outside of the home. As a result of which I am extremely cautious about what I eat and from whom I eat.

I really could not recall eating anything outside, the only place I had eaten was from home. However, I still could not believe that Miss Williams would be trying to hurt me in such a way. We had no physical disagreement. What I noticed, however, was that she was developing her little attitude here and there but everything on the surface seemed to be all right. At least I really wanted everything to be all right. We both attended the same church and even sat together in the same pew. Looking at both of us walking into the house of God every Sunday morning no one would ever believe that she had a diabolical plot against my life?

A few months after moving into the new place my Aunt Cynthia who resided in New Jersey passed away so we had a family gathering. I praise God that my aunt took her last breath calling on the name of Jesus. One of my cousins, Cislyn traveled from Jamaica to attend her mom's funeral. At that time she was filled with the Holy Spirit.

COURAGE UNDER FIRE!!

We stood under the New Jersey stars and talked about our God for hours. We were so connected in the spirit that when she asked if she could stay with me in Brooklyn for the summer I was thrilled. I rarely had visitors because of my hectic schedule so I was very excited to say the least. When I informed Miss Williams about my cousin's impending visit her attitude got worse. However, that did not deter me from having my cousin visiting for the mere fact that I had never objected to her having visitors.

One night in my dream I saw a very fierce alligator lurching out of a river and it was barking viciously like a dog. In the dream the river was in our kitchen. I took note of it but kept going. In my heart I knew that fiery trials were coming but like most Christians I saw it, knew it was not a good dream but never prayed with the fierceness that I should have and rebuked it. My spiritual eyes were still not quite opened to the depth of ugliness that exists in the dark world. God speaks to His children through dreams and this was definitely a warning. It was not to scare me but what I needed to have done was to pray defensively. Whatever is in the spirit will eventually manifest in the physical and that was exactly what was about to happen.

The following week Cislyn came to Brooklyn. When she met Miss Williams she started asking me if everything was all right and where did I meet this lady. I remember saying that we get along for the most part, however, of late it seems like something is really not right. I said to her that I can't quite put my finger on it, but lately there was a growing underlying tension. Cislyn did not have much to say but she had a look of concern on her face. In retrospect I realized that she was not only concerned but was also interceding for me and for herself. What she discerned then was that her cousin was living with no ordinary roommate.

She came to America to attend her mom's funeral and to get some rest before returning to the classroom but obviously God had a different plan. Part of which was to help prepare me for the fight of my life. Upon my cousin's arrival Miss Williams was making it very clear that she had a very ungodly agenda concerning me. Miss Williams became very restless. The Holy Spirit urged me to look for the black underwear she had given me a year ago. It was nowhere to be found. I looked in every corner in my bedroom. I moved my chess just in case it fell in between the drawers but still no sign of it. Through all of this I was very calm only because of my faith in God.

Hebrews 11:6 says "Without faith it is impossible to please God and he that comes to him must believe that he is and that he is a rewarder of those who diligently seek him." I did not fully understand the reason behind her behavior but I trust the God in whom I serve.

"CHALLENGES ARE STEPPING STONES TO THE THRONE ROOM OF GOD"

Sheron M. Clarke

CHAPTER THREE

TESTING AND TRIALS

Beloved, think it not strange concerning the fiery trial which is to try you, as though some strange thing happened unto you. I Peter 4:12.

   After my cousin came and summed up the situation she said "It seems like God has called you for spiritual warfare, well, better you than me." I asked her "What is spiritual warfare?" All I wanted to do was mind my own business in America but then who am I to tell God how to mold me and fashion me for His Kingdom? We are either surrendered vessels or we are not and I had made up my mind from the beginning that I was not going to live half heartedly for God. The truth of the matter is if I were playing church this woman would have taken me out in the spirit before my cousin even got here. My cousin coming to spend time with me was nothing short of God's providence to help open my eye to the realm of spiritual warfare.

   There was no real teaching about spiritual warfare in my church so my cousin gave me some instructions as to how to use my weapon. She encouraged me to stay constantly in the word of God. She encouraged me to read Psalm 51 everyday. She also said when the arrows come to send them back to sender and plead the Blood of Jesus Christ over my life. I thank God for the spirit of obedience that is in me because I took every instruction literally. Little did I know that it would later make a difference between life and death, sickness and health, insanity and sanity, poverty and wealth. I was in the Holy Spirit school and this was not theory but practical learning up close and personal.

COURAGE UNDER FIRE!!

There was never a certainty as to whether Miss Williams was in the house or not. There were times it felt and sounded like she was in her bedroom but she was not there physically because later she would come through the front door. She went to Jamaica once for about a week. The following Saturday morning at about 7:00 am I heard the screen door opened then the front door. I turned over and continued sleeping, thinking she has returned from her trip. An hour or so later Miss Williams opened the door and came walking up the stairs. I asked my cousin if she did not hear Miss Williams come in earlier. My cousin said yes she heard the door opened earlier but what she did was to send her spirit ahead of her.

By now I had moved up from half a day fasting to twenty-four hours. Once I was in prayer seeking the face of the Lord prior to breaking my first twenty-four hour fast. It was about midnight and when I was about to put the kettle on the stove a force knocked it out of my hand and instinctively I knew that I needed to continue the fast. I stood there thinking, what's next? I knew something was about to happen but did not know from where or how. I went to the front door to put the night lock on when I sense a whole host of demons were there. The Lord was taking me to another level in spiritual warfare. That was the first time I started bracing myself and literally throwing punches like Mike Tyson when faced with evil of this magnitude. I became vicious in the spirit and kept repeating the word of God until they backed off. The scent of sulfur was so strong that I felt nauseated as I stood at the front door. I locked the door and went to bed.

Obviously, she was not trying to hide her motives or to be subtle anymore. The spiritual battle had now intensified. On weekends my cousin would visit her sister-in- law who lives in Queens, New York. For some reason Miss Williams always seemed to want to pick a fight with me on a Sunday morning prior to going to church. The Enemy was also using her to try and distract me from absorbing the word of God. She would often start an argument on a Sunday morning. I believe this was done in order to deliberately disturb my spirit so that it would take everything in me to concentrate on the service. This was all the time.

A characteristic of the Enemy is to distract the people of God from growing in the word of God. Have you ever noticed that you will watch television for four to five hours, some folks even longer and the moment you take up the Bible you start snoring? If you are not snoring you are thinking of what to eat or what you will be wearing to work in the morning. Or your thoughts would be on five or more other things that have nothing to do with reading the Bible. He does it to all of us. How you overcome this is to recognize that he is behind the scheme and resolve in your heart that you will not be denied the benefits and blessings that God has for you in His word.

Another strategy of his is that you will be exiting church after hearing a great message or the choir sang a song that resonated in your spirit only to walk in a customized test just for you. We need to be cognizant of the devises of the Enemy. In Ephesians 5:15 it says "See then that you walk circumspectly, not as fools but as wise, redeeming the time, because the days are evil." He does not care who you are or where you are. You can be sitting in the pulpit and be sinning in your thoughts. That is why we are warned to walk circumspectly. Be watchful over what enters your mind and what you allow to linger.

The agents of Satan are always talented people. They are usually very good singers or teachers because this is how they get to infiltrate the church by serving in some leadership capacity. Miss Williams was never thrilled about being on the choir but she would do solos. She sang soprano beautifully.

Early one Sunday morning as I was cleaning the chicken she was leaving the kitchen going up the stairs. I told her that she has such a beautiful voice and that she really needs to repent and use it for God. She turned around with a speed that was not normal, given her age and ran up into my face a couple inches away blowing very hard. The Holy Spirit, the same One who had knocked the kettle out of my hand earlier, knocked the knife out of my hand and it landed out of both our reach. I stood firm and looked her in the face and shouted "The Blood of Jesus!" She jumped back as if I had physically shoved her. I repeated "The Blood of Jesus!" She started really backing up and saying "Watch here, watch here, watch here, watch the likle pickney" which in our local dialect means the little child.

She thought she could overpower me because in her mind I was a baby in Christ. I am convinced that she was on an assignment from the pit of hell. She knew that there was a mark that God had placed upon me even though I did not know it at the time. God has a strange way of bringing out the gifts and callings that He has placed in us and He uses many different methods to do this. Mine was Miss Williams and, yes, there were others but she was the main character in this long running episode. This war went on for over a decade even after we parted ways.

One night I came in from work and after which I had a business meeting so I was very tired at the end of a long day. I heard my cousin praying "Oh God, cover, cover, cover Oh God." I was really tired so I started praying but then I fell asleep. While sleeping I dreamt that I was walking toward the kitchen when I saw a lady standing at the sink. She was in a church dress and had on a hat that was perched on the top of her unprocessed hair. She was older than Miss Williams but she looked just like her only that her complexion was darker. I kept walking toward her because she was in a church dress and so I thought she was a friend but when I got closer and she looked at me, the spirit of God in me got angry. I braced myself and started boxing like Mike Tyson in the dream and it was so forceful that I woke up fighting.

My cousin said firmly "Get on your knees and pray! pray! pray!" I jumped off the bed and fell on my knees and called out to God for deliverance from evil and from every trap that the Enemy has set for me. I knew that this woman in the dream was the spirit of Miss Williams' mother who had been dead for many years at that time. She often bragged about her parents having leadership position in the church and how she grew up in the church. What was this spirit doing in my kitchen in my dream only God knows but I knew it was not good.

I know that there are some people who do not believe that God speaks to His children through dreams. I would be a fool not to believe after all that I had experienced and after all the manifestations of those dreams. I had so many dreams during this ordeal. I remember one night I went to bed I kept seeing so many centipedes and creeping insects that I jumped out of my sleep and said this woman is trying to take my mind. My cousin shouted "Get on your knees and pray! pray! pray!"

All these incidents made me even hungrier for God. I could not get enough of God. I attended a Church of God denomination and in addition to fasting it was always emphasized that the members be filled with the Holy Spirit with the manifestation of speaking in tongues. I wanted this so badly especially since I was in intense warfare. At times, I would be speaking in my heavenly language in my dream but it would never come in the physical as hard as I would seek the Lord.

One day as I sought the Lord in my bedroom and was crying out to Him and worshipping, Miss Williams started making a lot of noise in her bedroom. She went as far as to turn up her radio very loud. She knew that my desire was to be filled with the Holy Spirit with the evidence of speaking in tongues as the Spirit gives utterance, so she was determined to block that also. Is anyone still wondering if she was on the Lord's side?

One morning while I was praying I felt as if someone used a piece of plank and hit me on the top of my head. I rubbed the area and continued praying. Another morning while in prayer I not only felt the hit but the Lord allowed me to see it in the spirit coming towards me and hitting me on the top of my head. It bounced off my head like a rubber ball and I did not feel the impact. Then did I realize that this was another channel she was using to throw spiritual blows at me. She was pulling out all the stops to try and cripple my walk with the Lord and also to damage me physically.

While the people of God are sleeping the wicked are trying to find ways to carry out their evil deeds. Another night while I was sleeping I saw in the spirit when this fat older man came over me to try and strangle me. I was lying on my back so I doubled my fists and boxed him away then turned over on my belly and continued to sleep. In the morning I asked the Lord "What was that last night?" In Ephesians 6: 12 it says "For we wrestle not against flesh and blood, but against principalities, against powers, against the rulers of the darkness of this world, against spiritual wickedness in high places." Satan does not give up. He is relentless in his quest to destroy the people of God and he will use whomsoever is available even if they sit beside you in the pew or you live in the same house. It was constant warfare almost every night.

When you are a target of the Enemy warfare is not confined to only one area of your life. Not only was it in my home but also on my job. I worked at a bank and I was placed in a certain department with a very nice supervisor. He was very knowledgeable, kind and helpful. He realized that there was a conspiracy to make my work life miserable. This went on for several months until he had witnessed enough. He came in one morning and called a team meeting, excluding me. He warned my coworkers to treat me better or else they would all be written up. Their attitude and behavior toward me improved and that was the end of that episode. God then used me in their midst to be the peacemaker on the team. God has a way of turning situation around in such a way that you have to wonder if these were the same people who wanted to bury you alive just the other day.

This is why when we are being tried we have to be very careful that we do not tarnish our witness. They need to see Christ in us even under severe pressure. I am not saying it is easy because all of us can think of tests that came and we did not do so well in the furnace. However, after walking with the Lord for a while we should gain inner strength to withstand more pressure.

One of the things I did to avoid the conflict at home and to get a break from the constant spiritual attacks was to spend as little time as possible home. Many nights I would be going home 12:00 midnight or 1:00 am in the morning spending as little time as possible in that environment. I hardly slept because my spirit was always ready for anything and at anytime. I had bags underneath my eyes. I was constantly fasting so I was thin but through it all I was never sickly and in bed for any reason. When the attacks came and I did not feel well in my body God would quickly and supernaturally heal me.

Our enemies can be a blessing in disguise because they either pull us away from God or draw us closer to Him. I made up in my mind that I was going to get closer to my God. I knew that there was something that the Enemy was trying to keep me from receiving from my Lord and Savior. However, I was determined to get it, come what may. I was willing to pay the price for this great treasure even at the risk of every skin coming off my knees. If that were to happen my plan was to lay flat on my face all the time before God but I was not going to be deterred. With every attack I got hungrier for more spiritual food.

One evening as I opened the door I saw thick cloud or vapor of smoke sauntering through the living room and the kitchen. I said to myself "Did she leave something on the stove?" But as I walked closer trying to pick up the scent of possibly food burning, the smoke got less and less. Nothing was on the stove. I said "God, what is this?" I had never heard anybody in church testifying of these things so I kept my mouth shut. This happened again on another occasion so I asked my cousin who by then was back in Jamaica what could this mean. Her explanation was that whatever Miss Williams did in the house to hurt me that the glory (Holy Spirit) of God was neutralizing it. She said you are so protected that she cannot hurt you. I thank God for His hedge of protection that He has around His children. In the book of Exodus 13:21 the Bible says that the Lord went before the children of Israel by day in a pillar of cloud to lead the way, and by night in a pillar of fire to give them light; to go by day and night.

COURAGE UNDER FIRE!!

The Enemy is never out of ideas as to how he can terrorize the people of God. As I left my home to go to work one morning I felt as if a whole group of people were trying to push me to the ground. I could feel the forces of darkness and all I had to do to keep from falling on my face was to repeat the scripture "I shall not die but live, and declare the works of the Lord. I shall not die but live and declare the works of the Lord." Psalm 118:17. I kept repeating this over and over again until when I got to the next block the pressure lifted. The Bible says resist the devil and he will flee from you James 4:7b. Little did I know that God was preparing me to declare His word.

"CHAMPIONS ARE NOT BUILT OVERNIGHT"

Sheron M. Clarke

CHAPTER FOUR

THE VALLEY OF THE SHADOW OF DEATH

Yea, thou I walk through the valley of the shadow of death, I will fear no evil; for thou art with me; thy rod and thy staff they comfort me. Psalm 23:4

The next summer my cousin came back to the States and the spiritual war was still raging. Miss Williams upon being told that my cousin was coming again to visit during the summer kept saying "No, not another summer, no, not another summer." My cousin came and it was one incident after another, nothing new. We fasted on Wednesdays and Sundays as was our custom then and still is today. We prayed together and we worshipped God. There was no physical confrontation because we believe in walking in the spirit and love of God. Romans 12:18 says "If it be possible, as much as lieth in you, live peaceably with all men."

She started telling her children that my cousin and I were working obeah against her. We thought that was so funny that we really had a good laugh over her accusation. When satanic agents cannot overpower you they always think that you are engaged in the same evil behavior that they are involved in. What puzzles them is that your source is more powerful than theirs yet they still refuse to accept the fact that your connection is only to Jesus Christ and Him alone.

Miss Williams' major problem was that we the children of God were walking in the spirit, not in the flesh. My cousin and I were on one accord, we had the same determination, faith and spiritual tenacity and we knew that demons must bow to the Christ in us. We were so on one accord that one morning when we woke up we were describing a similar dream in detail that we both had the same night and it involved Miss Williams. Miss Williams was living in hell on earth because the Bible says one can put a thousand to flight and two can put ten thousand to flight. The demons in her did not know what to do with each other and so she was in turmoil. But all she had to do was repent of her evil ways and call upon the Name of Jesus but instead her heart got harder – just like Pharaoh's.

The attacks will affect every area of your life; your body, your mind, your relationships, your job, your business and your finances. It was very difficult to find a place and my finances were also in turmoil. I had a special bag that I would keep my sales from my business and the Lord kept telling me to anoint my moneybag. Prior to this I never really had issues with finances and it never occurred to me to pray over my money. Miss Williams loved to use the products that I sold and so once she credited $80.00 worth of products. She was taking a very long time to pay so I asked her for the money. She looked me in the face and told me that she already paid me. I knew it was a lie, she knew it was a lie but I really had no intentions of fighting over it so I let it go. I had so many clients, some of whom I would credit products. My finances were so tied up that I remember looking over the invoices and I had well over a $1,000 worth of products on credit. God had to literally allow me to find money on the street so that I could eat. This happened more than once just in case I was tempted to think it was a coincidence. What a Mighty God!

I got the olive oil and anointed my moneybag and prayed over it. I asked God to bless my efforts and to bless my customers so they would want to pay on time. There was an immediate improvement in my business. All the outstanding debts from my customers started coming in. I encourage every

COURAGE UNDER FIRE!!

Believer of Christ to pray over their checking account, savings account and every investment with their name on it. We should also ask God to protect us from the devourer of our finances, protection from every evil hand that will try to contaminate our prosperity and divine wisdom to spend according to God's will and for His Kingdom.

We knew that something had to give and so no matter what, we were determined to find an apartment before the summer was out. We tried several places and during our search we went to this home that was advertised in the local newspaper. It was a walk -in apartment that was being rented. Upon entering the premises, on the right there was a porch that had a partition dividing the owners section from that which was being rented. The porch had burglar bars all around it and on the owner's side there was a big black dog that kept barking at us as we entered.

At first nothing seemed strange because my mind was on the apartment more than this dog that kept barking. I was praying and asking the Lord to confirm that this was where He wanted me to be. I desperately wanted to move from where I was living so my spiritual antennas were on high alert. After examining the place we stepped outside underneath the trees to talk as the owner asked me how I felt about what I had seen. I said to her I was still thinking about it and would give her a call to let her know. We were engrossed in the conversation but the dog's bark was so vicious that it penetrated my spirit. It seemed as if the dog wanted to rip the bars apart to eat us alive.

In one sharp movement I turned around in the direction of the dog and sternly asked the lady "What's its name?" She said that his name was Satan. Surprised by her answer, I asked her why would she give her dog such a name. She said that it was just a name that it did not mean anything and that it was not a big deal because after all it was only a name. I told her that names do have meaning, especially this name. I thanked her for her time and left knowing that I would never return. Our name is our identity and the Bible said that my people perish because of a lack of knowledge Hosea 4:6. There are some animals that people have as pets in their homes that are carrying some dangerous spirits. This was one such example.

We continued our search and we eventually found an apartment two blocks from where I was living. The lease was signed and my cousin and I could hardly wait for the move in date as we were both very elated. We were so very thankful to God. That evening I went on to my business meeting and Cislyn started cooking some soup. Prior to this we hardly cooked and had no desire to keep food in the house.

That evening while her soup was simmering she decided to take a shower. She said at about 6: 30 pm while she was in the shower she felt a cool breeze and the bathroom door became ajar. This was strange because there were no windows in the bathroom. She pulled back the shower curtain, closed the door and resumed taking her shower. She then felt a weird sensation and she knew that she was definitely not alone. She said she felt the hair standing on end all over her body. So she jumped out of the shower in time to see a dark shadow scurrying down the stairs. She ran behind it speaking the word of God and rebuking it in the Name of Jesus. She opened the front door and sent him right back to sender in the Name of Jesus.

When she related the incident to me I was somewhat relieved that someone else experienced what I was going through on a regular basis. Even though she was there with me this was her first one on one encounter. She said she, of course, knew what was going but this was just too unbelievable. She said to make matters worse this was 6:30 pm, in the evening, not midnight. We were even more anxious and excited at the same time that I was finally moving out and away from Miss Williams. Oh what a joy! The day seemed like it was taking forever. But finally it came and my ordeal was going to be over – at least so I thought.

On the night of my move it so happened that Miss Williams had gone to visit another church that Friday evening. She loves to go to church. These agents of Satan love to go to the house of God. They always find a church that they can plant themselves in and eventually destroy it if there are no strong Intercessors on the prayer wall. Sometimes the church struggles to move forward in the things of God because of these agents. They will sit in the spirit on the leaders, the members and the church's finance. Sometimes the church will become so lethargic that they are ineffective for God. In Revelation chapter 3:15-16 it says "I know thy works, that thou art neither cold nor hot: I would thou wert cold or hot. So then because thou art lukewarm, and neither cold nor hot, I will spue thee out of my mouth."

My brothers, my sister and another cousin came to Brooklyn to help me move. I was so happy to be moving and also for the fact that Miss Williams was nowhere around. When we were almost finished she came and you should have seen the expression on her face. It was obvious that her intentions were for me to stay there so she could overpower me and render me useless to God and to myself. The Enemy does not give up easily. It is only the people of God who tires easily when in battle. We whine and complain and act as if God has forgotten us or has lost His power.

When she came she went into her room for a while and when she emerged she offered me the kitchen table set we had purchased together. It was really not my taste. My cousin thought that I should take it and I understood her reason but I should not have. Be aware, this is how they tract you in the spirit by giving you something that they can attach themselves to.

On that same night in the summer of 1996 when I moved into my new apartment I started laying some linoleum between the bedroom and the bathroom. While I was on my knees I felt a warm sensation on the back of my legs. When I turned around and looked at my leg I saw blood coming from a small incision on my left leg. I wondered how this could have happened. I kept retracing my steps in my mind and knew that I did not hit my legs neither did I lift any heavy objects. I simply wiped away the blood and kept working. Knowing what I know now I would have prayed intentional and strategic warfare prayers against the attack of the enemy. After that incident I realized that this should not have been taken so lightly because after that there was one mark or another appearing on my legs. The Spirit of God prompted me to place my hand over my legs, plead the Blood of Jesus Christ over them and command that no more marks appear on my legs. That was the end of that.

We have authority in the Name of Jesus to declare a thing by faith and watch it manifest. Blood is significant in the spiritual world. Without the shedding of blood there can be no remission of sin. Everything that God does Satan tries to duplicate it. The life of the flesh is in the blood and so Jesus Christ was that sacrificial Lamb whose Blood had to be shed so that we could enjoy eternal life. He shed His Blood for our sin as a covenant that we are no longer under bondage to sin, if we accept Him as Lord and Savior of our lives.

COURAGE UNDER FIRE!!

The shedding of Jesus Christ's Blood is the atonement for our sin because God the Father requires it as payment. This was done on the cross so that we may have eternal life. If you have never asked Jesus Christ into your heart by confessing your sins and acknowledging that He shed His Blood just for you then now is a good time to do that. All you have to do is speak it by faith and believe in your heart that Jesus Christ died for you and that He rose from the grave. Ask forgiveness for your sins and you have just entered into a relationship with Jesus Christ. This could only have been possible because He shed His precious Blood for you on the cross over 2,000 years ago.

Satan on the other hand is an imitator and his purpose is not for our good. People operating in the dark world know that there is great significance attached to the shedding of the Blood of Jesus Christ. That is why they will often times sacrifice animals or even humans in their ritualistic practice to gain power from their master, Satan. If they can get access to your blood then they can afflict you in the spirit.

I know that there are skeptics out there who might be thinking oh well you are making too much out of nothing. But I can assure you that this is for real. So many times as Christians the devil is right up in your face, in your homes, in your children's lives but you do not recognize him until it is too late. Only then do you start crying and wondering what ever happened to your nice little girl or nice little boy. By the time you are asking what happened usually the damage has already been done. Relationships have been torn apart and you wonder what had gotten into this child. Well, I am here to tell you that the signs were there all along but you simply ignored the signs or refused to believe that the Enemy is real. Or you believe that it could only happen to someone else or someone else's children, but not yours.

COURAGE UNDER FIRE!!

On Friday December 14, 2012 a twenty year old gunman entered Sandy Hook Elementary School in Newtown, Connecticut and killed himself along with 27 others including his mother. Twenty of those murdered were children. Everyone is asking how could this have happened and of course everyone is looking for answer as to why. Unfortunately, the signs were there all along but they were not recognized for what it was. This is sheer demonic. We cannot fight spiritual battles with medication and on the other hand if you do need medication take it. No one recognized the depth of the spiritual darkness that was brewing in this young man's soul over the years. We are in a real war and we have to be spiritually vigilant over our children.

I met a young lady at a bus stop one day with a beautiful eight month old baby girl in her arms. I introduced myself to her and we scheduled an appointment for me to come to her home to demonstrate my products. When I went to her home she also had a toddler who was close to two years. They were both in diapers. I noticed that she had to be constantly snatching the eight month old baby away from the older one because the toddler was beating on the younger baby. Eventually when the child was taken away she jumped upon the couch that I was sitting on and raised her hand to slap me in my face. I caught her hand just in time and held it mid air. When I looked into the child's face I said to myself "This is not just a baby." I looked intently at her and she moved away. Soon afterwards the doorbell rang and it was a social worker coming to have sessions with this child who was not even talking properly. The social worker kept saying "Do not hit, don't hit". I thought to myself that this child needs some deep prayer.

This is an example of a child who was already being tormented by the devil. Whatever the root cause of her problem, whether it is psychological, hormonal imbalance, sociological or spiritual she needs deliverance prayer. In other words, prayer works no matter what the root of the problem is. If not dealt with properly in the spirit it will manifest into a bigger problem as she grows. Babies are not exempt from Satan. Anoint your children, pray over them and speak the word of God in their ears. In II Corinthians 10: 4- 5 it says "For the weapons of our warfare are not carnal, but mighty through God to the pulling down of strong holds; casting down imaginations; and every high thing that exalteth itself against the knowledge of God, and bringing into captivity every thought to the obedience of Christ."

In consistently working my cosmetics business, I was blessed to finally achieve my goal of being at the first level of management. Our meeting that night was quite a celebration that turned into a worship service. We gave God thanks for everything and I also encouraged my peers by ensuring them that they too could achieve this status with God by their side, hard work and perseverance.

In the midst of the celebration another church sister whom I had recruited on my team came over to congratulate me. She opened both arms and encircled my entire body. She squeezed me and rocked me from side to side for about a minute that seemed longer. When she released me I felt so dirty. I kept thinking to myself what on earth was that all about. She then turned to me and asked me if I could lend her my black jacket to attend a function since I would not be needing it any longer for the business. In this business when you are promoted the color of your jacket changes.

Before thinking twice I answered yes. A few days after the incident the Holy Spirit kept prompting me about her behavior. The more I thought about it the angrier I was feeling in my spirit so I knew that something was terribly wrong. I saw her in church and I asked her for my jacket. She promised to get it to me but it was not forthcoming. She lived about two blocks from the church and she kept forgetting to bring it and made no effort to get it after service was dismissed. It took her weeks after several requests to finally return the jacket. When she returned it I threw it in my closet knowing not to ever put it on my back again. The garment was spiritually contaminated and thanks to God I did not wear it. However, it should never have come inside my home. When I threw it in the closet all the demons that were on it were released. I could see them as rats running in the spirit throughout my home. I called my cousin and explained to her what had happened and what I had seen and she said they are demons, get rid of the jacket. I threw it in the dumpster and sent back every attack of the Enemy against me.

I immediately knew that this one was coming from this sister and not Miss Williams. In Psalm 24: 3-4 It says "Who shall ascend into the hill of the Lord? Or who shall stand in his holy place? He that hath clean hands and a pure heart: who hath not lifted up his soul to vanity, now sworn deceitfully." How could so many people in the house of God hands be so dirty?

It was really never a habit of mine to lend my clothes to anyone but because of the sisterhood in the organization I did it without thinking twice. This is why it is very important that we pray and ask the Lord to help us to keep our spiritual guards up all the time, even during celebration. There are people who operate in a deep level of witchcraft that they can control you if your guard is down. I was so happy and in deep celebration that I was taken off guard. That is why Ephesians 6:11 warns us to put on the whole armor of God, that we may be able to stand against the wiles of the devil. When you are a target you have to be totally dependent on the Holy Spirit because you never know how or where the Enemy will rear its ugly head.

I had this beautiful mirror on my wall 24" x 28"and one evening when I got home it was on the floor and shattered to pieces. Was it a coincidence? Maybe but I think not. One of the lessons I learned through this ordeal is that evil spirits can also channel themselves in your home through mirrors and crystals. I still had no fear but in my heart I knew that there was more to it. I thought moving would have changed things but I knew in my heart that it definitely was not over. I said to myself this obviously is part three because this was my third home since I first laid eyes on Miss Williams.

I later learned however that people who are this evil have the ability to transfer themselves through various channels into your home. They can gain access to your home through gifts that they have given you. Evil spirits can channel themselves through art that you bought from even a total stranger. If that person has evil intentions and did incantations over it what just happened is that they would have released and attached demonic spirits to that object. It can be your hair, clothing, jewelry, artwork, money or whatever the object happens to be.

A friend of mine, Elaine, her sister was blessed with a painting from one of her friends. It was a beautiful painting so she brought it home and proudly hung it on her living room wall. Shortly afterwards she started having nightmare every night where she was fighting with a group of people. It was the same people fighting her in her sleep every night. One night in her dream while she was fighting she asked one of the women where did she come from. She said the woman's response was that she invited them there. She still could not figure out why she was having this repeated dream regularly or who were these people.

One day another friend came to her home, saw the painting and asked her where did she get it from. She said it was a gift from someone who brought it back from Egypt. The person told her that it is not a good painting to have in her home because there were inscriptions on it that were ungodly to say the least. She then went over to the painting and looked keenly at it. That was when she realized that the same people she was fighting in her dream were the same people in the painting. She took the painting out of the frame and tried to burn it but it would not burn. She then took it outside and soaked it in kerosene oil and it eventually burned. Take careful note of every piece of furnishing or ornament that you take into your home and what you also wear.

I was always expecting anything and at anytime. I came home one night at about 11:00 pm to find that the lock on my front door had been totally removed. It was as if someone used a surgeon's scalpel and professionally cut out the entire lock leaving a huge hole in my door. When the police came they entered my apartment in search of the intruder who apparently was long gone. I had gift baskets lining my hallway but apparently they wanted cash that I rarely kept at home. After this incident I started putting a chair underneath the lock for extra security when I was home.

This night in particular I put the chair underneath the door handle and went to the bathroom. While I was in the bathroom I heard the chair moved. It made a thud as if someone opened the door and the chair fell. I came out of the bathroom and looked toward the direction of the front door that I could not see because of the design of the apartment. Then I thought to myself there is no way that could have happened. The chair was securely jammed underneath the knob. When I went back into the bathroom I felt this eerie presence so I ran to my bedroom and got my bottle of consecrated olive oil.

When I ran to the door the spirit of fear was so overwhelming. My heart started beating very fast and the spirit of fear was so thick that you could almost cut it with a knife, if it were possible. I started saying Psalm 27:1-2 "The Lord is my light and my salvation whom shall I fear. The Lord is the strength of my life of whom shall I be afraid? When the wicked, even mine enemies and my foes, came upon me to eat up my flesh, they stumbled and fell" along with some other scriptures. The feeling was still very strong and the presence I felt would not budge. I started rebuking and binding and I stood my ground in the Name of Jesus but I could still sense this scary, eerie presence. When I started speaking in my heavenly language that was when I felt the presence getting weaker and weaker until they eventually left. I knew that the war had intensified even more.

There were nights I felt nauseas and sick to my stomach and I would pray and anoint myself with the oil representing the Holy Spirit according to James 5:14 committing myself to the Lord. I would say to the Lord that my life is in His hands and asked Him to wash me in His precious Blood. The next morning I would wake up feeling great as if nothing had happened the previous night. There were times I had to pinch myself to feel if I was still alive, confirming that I had made it through another night. There were also many times I wondered if this was going to be my last night.

Experiences like these set you apart and can make you feel very isolated. It is a very lonely journey. Very few people will admit to having experiences like this because they are afraid of being ridiculed or called crazy. Even the very church folks who claim to be "spiritually deep" will look at you strange and talk negatively behind your back. Our Sunday night services were usually dismissed about 12:00 midnight and sometimes even later. The leader of the Missionary Ministry gave me a ride home one night. When I got to my home she said "Sister Sheron, you look so pretty in your dress go in to your duppy (ghost)." She thought it was very funny and she laughed so hard that all I could do was look at her, smiled and thanked her while getting out of her vehicle.

In the beginning I would share my dreams and some of my experiences in testimony service but my cousin advised me to stop so that ended quickly. She said "Sheron, many people who are even in leadership position in the church have not seen half the things that you have experienced and you just really started walking with the Lord." This was shocking to me because I thought this was something that every Christian had to experience in order to get to the next level in their walk with God. I really thought it was a normal process due to the fact that immediately after rededicating my life to the Lord the battles started happening. I did not get a chance to enjoy even a week of Christian bliss this time around.

My cousin explained to me that my calling was different. This is what she referred to earlier as spiritual warfare. It was a constant time of learning to fight, absorbing, resting in the Lord, reading the word and doing more fighting. Life already has its challenges that we all have to deal with on a daily basis. However, when spiritual arrows are constantly being sent your way by various people (enemy and "friends") that is when life can seem unbearable. I resolved in my heart not to worry about what others think. I was determined to live through this and to give God all the glory. What I did, however, was to limit those with whom I share my daily experiences.

COURAGE UNDER FIRE!!

When we know Him in an intimate way one of the lessons we must learn is how to walk alone. There will be a season in our training when there is no one to talk to. The Enemy cannot touch us unless he gets permission from God and this will be granted in order to help us to grow. For us to be highly effective in the spirit realm, the Holy Spirit teaches us to learn to rely on Him more than we do people. Yes, we all need encouragement and everyone needs to feel that there is someone on earth who is in his corner but the Holy Spirit has a way of teaching us that He is our Sustainer, He is our Comforter and He is our Guide and a Friend who sticks closer than a brother.

He will allow friends to betray and abandon us so that we can know Him in a way we never could with friends whom we call upon for everything. We have a tendency to call upon friends in times of trouble before remembering that we have not prayed. We will email, phone, facebook, text and tweet all our issues which oftentimes will come back to bite us before calling upon that One who is a true Friend.

So many people are lonely and it does not matter what their status in life is; rich, poor, married or single. I believe that the worse kind of loneliness is to be in a relationship and still feel the pangs of loneliness. There is a difference between being alone and lonely. One can be alone and be at peace and have more joy than someone who has a lot of people around them yet is totally miserable in his spirit. Such peace and joy comes from within and that is what the Holy Spirit teaches us. In Hebrews 13:5 His promise is that He will never leave us nor forsake us. How will we know Him as a Friend if we never spend time alone with Him? If it were up to us we would never choose this path. However, He allows us to go through this because it is another part of the process to increase our faith in Him.

COURAGE UNDER FIRE!!

Jesus Christ felt the pangs of loneliness as He hung on the cross for our sins. He cried "E'-li E'-li, la'-ma sa-bach'-than-ni?" that is to say, My God, my God why has thou forsaken me? Matthew 27:46. There is no pain that you will go through that the true and living God cannot relate to. He felt them all while He walked on earth among us. He also knows what it is like to feel tired, weary, hungry, thirsty, rejected, beaten, humiliated and betrayed.

There was a season when friends had either betrayed me, misunderstood me or was nowhere to be found. During this time of isolation I also could not feel God. It felt as if my prayers were hitting a brass ceiling. This went on for a season but I never stopped praying and seeking the face of God. In the beginning I did not understand why I could not feel Him anymore but as I persevered I realized that He was teaching me that He was not just a feeling. He was with me whether I felt Him or not because that was His promise to me. He was teaching me to trust Him no matter what I was going through. If we have never needed a friend how would we have known God as a true Friend who sticks closer than a brother? How would we know Him as One who will walk through the storm with us? Know that it is all a test and once we have passed a test there is another one waiting. This is how we are elevated in the spirit realm.

Nevertheless, the Lord has a way of encouraging His people in the darkest hour. He will give you glimpses of where He wants to take you to strengthen you. One night He showed me a group of women dressed in long white dress and white headdress. They were on their knees with their faces to the ground. I knew in my heart that God was showing me a vision of what was to come. I asked the Lord where were these women coming from. I knew it was a special prayer ministry that He was going to birth through me but I had to be processed for the task. This was His way of encouraging me to hold on to His unchanging hand in the darkness.

Once I remember sharing a little of what I was going through with a friend and neighbor whom I had known from Montego Bay, Jamaica. When I was a backslider she was a Christian who wore no jewelry, no processed hair, no makeup, she was in church it seems twenty four seven. After sharing a little of what I was going through with her she had such fear on her face. Then she asked me "Are you going home tonight?" To which I responded "Where else should I go?" "I must go home." All I had to hold on to was the word of God. In Isaiah 41:10 it says "Fear thou not; for I am with thee: be not dismayed; for I am thy God: I will strengthen thee; yea, I will help thee; yea, I will uphold thee with the right hand of my righteousness."

I knew that God was with me through the dark experiences. One of the attacks of the Enemy is to hinder the word of God from taking root in the heart of His people. I had to struggle and be intentional that I would remember scriptures. I knew it was demonically based because I have a good memory and not for the life of me could I remember Bible verses. I also had a problem when I was called upon to lead a chorus at church. I would go blank and every song would leave my mind immediately. A determination rose up on the inside of me once I realized that this was another tactic of the Enemy. John 10:10 states the Enemy comes but to rob, kill, steal and destroy. Some things do not just happen they are designed by the Enemy to rob us of the purpose of God in our lives and our destiny. This verse continues to say that Jesus came that we might have life and have it more abundantly. I chose to remember scriptures and to be able to sing before the people of God for His glory.

COURAGE UNDER FIRE!!

As I knelt to pray at the church alter one night I said to God, "Lord I am not afraid but I am tired and I know that you are with me but please show me a sign that you are." Before I could finish speaking the Lord showed me a man dressed in bright, white satin outfit with red borders around the sleeves and the legs. He was sitting on the couch as if to say "I got you." His two hands were sprawled out on the back of my couch and he just spread out on it as if he owned it and He did. This was Isaiah 65:24 "And it shall come to pass, that before they call, I will answer; and while they are yet speaking, I will hear."

From that day every time I passed the couch I would imagine the angel of the Lord sitting there protecting me. That gave me even more comfort as I continued to walk through the valley of the shadow of death because His word continues to say that He is with me and that His rod and His staff they comfort me.

Prayer
Restrict and
Eradicate
Satan's strategies and
Strongholds

Cislyn Cole

CHAPTER FIVE

HIS UNSEEN HAND

…I am the Lord; I will bring you out from under the burdens of the Egyptians, and I will rid you out of their bondage, and I will redeem you with a stretched out arm, and with great judgments: Exodus 6:6

Through this ordeal I never wavered in my faith. I just kept asking God "What is this, what is going on?" "Why me?" All I wanted to do was to come to America like everyone else and enjoy the "American dream". I had no idea that these occurrences could happen. I always thought they were old wives tales, folk story, hallucination, indigestion, but not real.

I remember walking to church one night and talking to God both of which I did very often. I asked God "What is it that is in me that the Enemy is trying so hard to kill?" I really wanted to know. I thought to myself that there must be someone else out there who could relate to what was happening in my life apart from my cousin to whom I am eternally grateful.

Apparently walking back and forth to church was drawing other people's attention including a madman who now seems to know when I would be passing a certain intersection. I am not referring to a clean looking mad person who had lost a few "screws". I am referring to someone who was jet black with dirt from head to toe and eyes red as blood. If I leave a little early he would be standing at a specific intersection. If I leave my home later he would be there or be just about getting there. I thought to myself how on earth would he know what time I would be passing.

One night as I stood at the intersection to cross over to the next side he approached me on my left trying to intimidate me. Wrong night! I had had enough of him, Miss Williams plus the others and I was not running. He stared at me and I turned my head toward him looking straight at him and daring him to come any closer. He stared at me for a brief moment, groaned then walked away. I said to him "Oh, you better." I had had enough of demons and I was ready to beat down anything that came in my way, spiritually or physically. Maybe at this moment you would call me crazy for challenging a mentally deranged demoniac but I choose to call it holy anger.

About a month after that incident I was walking home from church one Sunday afternoon and there he was again. I had passed the intersection and was a little distance away from him. Thankfully, it was daylight but this time he had a friend with him, another madman. I turned around to see and hear him complaining, in grunt like manner, to his friend and pointing at me. Have you ever seen a well-dressed woman running in heels? Well, if you did more than likely that was I. I made sure not to run directly home just in case they were following me. I later learned that the large building to the left across from the residential homes was the back of the G building (Psychiatric Ward) of Kings County Hospital. That was it. I changed my route.

Afterwards the Holy Spirit kept urging me to go to the bookstore. I was so thrilled to see books on witchcraft. I was so overjoyed to have in my possession books that talked about wickedness in the spiritual realm and books that I could identify with. We serve an awesome God who takes care of His children. We all have a path to travel and some of us have a more pleasant view than others. God allows us to have our experiences for a reason and I believe it is so that He will get the glory at the end, if we faint not.

Through all the spiritual encounters, I had never suffered from depression. I went to work everyday while at the same time building my cosmetic business. One cannot be dreary and do well in sales so looking back I am amazed at how God has kept me. I believe He did it this way so that I would never be tempted to take His glory or subdue His praise. Every breath that I take is an attribute to the God that I serve. Every time I inhale or exhale it is a tribute to God's grace and mercy.

The Spirit of God hedged me around on every hand. All I can say is that God protected me. He said in Psalm 139:5 "Thou has beset me behind and before, and laid thine hand upon me." The fight was on every side. By this time I knew that Miss Williams was definitely a ploy in the Enemy's hand. The fight was bigger than her. This was coming from the pit of hell and it seems as if he was determined to get me one way or another. I was also very determined to walk righteously before God because I know that there is no devil that is more powerful than the God that I serve.

As a result of all these challenges some would ask "Then if God is so powerful why didn't He stop the Enemy from doing all of these things to you?" My question to you would then be "How would I have known what spiritual gifts were in me if God did not allow me to go through the challenges?" Or better yet, "How would I have known how powerful and mighty my God is if I had never known Him as a Deliverer?" "How would Daniel truly know that God could shut the mouth of the lions if King Darius did not throw him in the den?" Talk is cheap and a lot of Christians talk the talk but are not willing to walk the walk. Yet sometime they criticize those who dare to step away from the shore and into the deep. All the great patriarchs were tested in some way or the other. So why do we think that we should not go through anything difficult. No, we must take up our cross daily. Everybody's cross is different. For some people it is their abusive husband or wife, some it is their wayward child, some it is poverty or lack, some it is an abrasive boss or supervisor. For some people it is all of the above but whatever the cross happen to be it is meant to increase our faith in God and give Him glory.

In 1999 I started experiencing a little difficulty when I swallowed my saliva. Due to the fact that there were so many challenges going on at the same time I put it on the back burner, so to speak. It got to the point where at times I would lift up my head from my pillow to be able to swallow more freely. A few days prior to leaving for Dallas on a business trip I anointed my throat and asked the Lord to heal me. As soon as we checked into the hotel my girlfriends and I hopped in a cab to attend the Wednesday night midweek service at the Potters House in Dallas. The minister's message was about the two fish and the five loaves taken from Matthew chapter 14. It was an anointed word in which he also spoke about totally surrendering to the will of the Lord for Him to use us however He chooses.

At the altar call I moved towards the front of the church crying unto the Lord for Him to use me for His glory. As I got closer a female minister briskly walked off the pulpit and stood in front of me. She put one hand on my throat and the other she held up to heaven and cried unto the Lord to heal me. My only reason for going to the altar was my hunger to get closer to God. At that time I was not thinking about my throat. I knew that something was not quite right in my throat but my hunger for God to use me was so great that it overshadowed everything else that was going on in my life. When she was crying out to God on my behalf for Him to heal me, I looked through my tears and said "Lord I want what she has." This minister of God was for real and very anointed. The Bible said that we should covet good gifts and so as we mature in our walk our discernment should get sharper. We should be more able to spot authentic anointing.

These are a few of the many benefits of being a child of God but we have to be walking in divine order. We cannot have sin in our lives and expect to walk in the depth of such anointing. Psalm 91:1 says "He that dwelleth in the secret place of the Most High shall abide under the shadow of the Almighty." In other words, Satan cannot come in the secret place to get us we have to venture out. Two things happened during this encounter at the altar: The Lord healed my throat and my craving for God was even more intensified.

Satan had to ask God for permission to attack Job because the hedge of protection was so thick around Job and his family. Why? Because scripture says Job was a righteous man. In Job 1:8 God gave Satan permission to touch his stuff but not his body. When Satan realized that Job was firm in his faith he made a second appearance before God to ask permission to attack his body. "Do you see how persistent Satan is to destroy the people of God?" God told Satan in Job 2:6 that Job was in his hand but to save his life. It became clear in my heart that what was happening to me was preparation for the purpose of God in my life.

At this point in my life I was thinking that God wanted to use me for some cause but I still was not thinking preaching in a pulpit. I was in love with Jesus and I wanted more and more of Him. I wanted more of Him so badly that the fiercer the battle raged the more determined I became to hold on tighter to Him. Whatever I was learning through spiritual warfare it was so I could get closer to Jesus Christ. All this warfare was intended

71

by the Enemy to get me to step away from the things of God. Maybe that tactic would work with someone else but all it did to me was to light a fire in my heart for God that is unquenchable. I was thoroughly enjoying my prayer life and worship experience.

Apparently, I was growing quite a bit because I met a sister once who came back and told me that she had to talk to her Pastor about me. I asked her about what. She said that every time she came into my presence all the hair stood up on her body. I was really shocked. She said her Pastor said either this lady is very wicked or she is very anointed. Thankfully, she said she told her Pastor that I was not wicked. God knows exactly what our needs are and so He has a way of sending the right people in our path to be a source of encouragement. This kind neighbor was such a one at that time. I could see the love of Jesus all over her so I shared a little about what was going on and she prayed for me.

One of the things I realized while going through my spiritual challenges was that not too many people want to pray for you or with you when you are going through such intense warfare. Not to mention coming into your home to pray for you. I do not hold that against them however because one has to be wise when it comes to conducting deliverance session. It is important that we seek the face of God to find out if we should go in the first place. Then you need to get instructions from the Holy Spirit as to how to operate under the anointing when you get there.

The reason I said that is because some people open spiritually dark doors and have no intention of living for Christ so we have to be wise where we go and in whose territory we are treading.

COURAGE UNDER FIRE!!

As I am writing the Enemy wants me to feel embarrassed because this is not a popular subject and he does not want to be further exposed. This is not a topic where you look like a hero and everything seems rosy and peachy. Nobody wants to look like they are constantly being challenged by the devil but he is a liar. In I Corinthians 1:27 it says "But God hath chosen the foolish things of the world to confound the wise; and God hath chosen the weak things of the world to confound the things which are mighty." This is so that no flesh should glory in his presence. I am willing to look foolish for my God anytime especially if it will deliver somebody.

So in all these events what God had been doing with me was to sharpen my spiritual eyes and ears. He purged my mind, body, spirit and soul. Everyday I was becoming more like Christ. It seemed like I was always going through a lot of challenges and yes it was true but the Holy Spirit was strengthening me on the inside for such a time as this. What was so surprising was that I did not look like my circumstances. The Lord God preserves His people. Shadrack, Meshach and Abednego were bound and thrown into a fiery furnace that was heated seven times its normal temperature. The temperature was so hot that it killed the men who threw them in. But the angel of the Lord went into the fire with Shadrack, Meshach and Abednego, walked and talked with them while they were in the furnace. The Bible said when they came out their hair was not singed, their clothes were in the same condition it was in before they were thrown in. The smell of smoke was not even on them. That is the awesomeness of our God. There is absolutely nothing that is too difficult for Him to do.

As Believers if we could just grasp the love and might of our God we would all live a more peaceful and surrendered life. At the time, all I wanted to do was to live a "normal" life but my

life is not my own. It belongs to God and when we say as
Christians we surrender all we better mean it because all means
everything. We serve a loving God and He knows what is best
for us. He says in Isaiah 59:19 "…When the enemy shall come
in like a flood, the Spirit of the LORD shall lift up a standard
against him."

In Isaiah 55:8 he says "For my thoughts are not your
thoughts neither are your ways my ways." God promises us also
that He will not give us more than we can bear. Sometimes it
seems as if we cannot go another step but God gives us grace to
not only make one more step but another and another until we
finish the mile. He says in Galatians 6:9 "And let us not be
weary in well doing: for in due season we shall reap if we faint
not." I encourage us all to pray without ceasing 1 Thessalonians
5:17.

"AT EVERY SIDE THERE IS THE BAPTISM OF THE SPIRIT OF SATANISM"

Sheron M. Clarke

CHAPTER SIX

DELIVERANCE FROM EVIL

Many are the afflictions of the righteous: but the LORD delivereth him out of them all. Psalm 34:19

In the midst of all these nightmare experiences I could see the mighty hand of God. The more I worshipped Him the closer He drew me to Him. The depth of our trial, determines the depth of our worship. I thank God for the experiences I have had because it was God's way of molding me and fashioning me to be more like Him. He used different methods for different people but depending on your purpose and your call He uses the various trials accordingly. This happens to be my journey but whatever the method, there will be spiritual warfare in our lives on some level. It is important, however, that we recognize it when it comes and know how to use our weapon. In Ephesians 6:11 it encourages us to put on the whole armor of God so that we will be able to stand against the wiles of the devil.

However, for us to be usable in the hand of God, He has to purge us. I know a lot of people think they have it all together but the Lord said in Isaiah 64:6 "But we are all as an unclean thing, and all our righteousness are as filthy rags; and we all do fade as a leaf; and our iniquities, like the wind, have taken us away." When we come into the presence of a Holy God we are a mess. That is why I thank God for the shed Blood of His Son Jesus Christ because that is what gives us access to the throne of grace. There is absolutely no other avenue though many would want to convince us otherwise.

The frequent attacks kept me on my guard at all times and so I would and still do today examine myself daily. I said to the

Lord that if there is any sin in me that I have not repented of to please forgive me. My constant prayer to the Lord is if there is anything in me that does not sit well with Him I want Him to please show me. Also if there is any spiritual misalignment in my life please reveal it to me. It does not have to be the sin of fornication, adultery, stealing or lies but our attitude or our whole demeanor could be so foul that we need to ask the Lord to show us the root cause of our disposition so we can repent. The little quirks in our lives that we ignore are sometimes the very things that break our fellowship with God. According to Solomon 2:15 … the little foxes that spoil the vines…..

To ensure that my heart was right concerning Miss Williams, one day I went to her and asked her to forgive me if I had hurt her. I searched my heart and I could not find anything but I said to myself just in case I missed it let me ask her. No one is above reproach so if I was guilty of anything I wanted to hear it from her mouth. Her response was "You have not done me anything." So I asked her "Why do you hate me?" She answered "I do not hate you." After that response I had nothing else to say to her. I left thinking that I had done my part and I will never fully understand the depth of her evil toward me. I also came to the conclusion that she was being driven by a dark, sinister force, Satan himself, and she now had no control over her actions.

Every word from our Lord and Savior Jesus Christ is to be taken literally. There is a reason for every request and for every command that He gave us. Jesus said in Mark 11: 26 "But if ye do not forgive, neither will your Father which is in heaven forgive your trespasses." An unforgiving heart is a devil's playground. If we hold grudges, unforgiveness, bitterness, anger, malice and resentment in our hearts against other people then we have given the Enemy legal right to come in and torment us and our loved ones. Christians who harbor unforgiveness in their heart will never get to the level in the spirit realm where God can fully use them for His glory. Their anointing will be contaminated and so they will not be very effective for God.

There are so many wonderful Believers who have been wounded by friends, family members or people in the church and because of that they are walking around with an infected heart. This spiritual wound can and oftentimes manifest in a physical illness because that is Satan's way of saying that he has shares in your body. We do not want him to even come near our dwelling place so one of the ways to keep him out is to forgive. It doesn't matter who is the guilty party, true freedom is forgiving no matter who is wrong. This is what is referred to as walking in the spirit because flesh cannot do that. This is a supernatural act and it can only happen through total surrender to the word and the will of God.

You will walk around with less baggage and the Enemy will find it very hard to clasp its poisonous tentacles around your heart. It means that you can command demons to flee and rebuke them in the name of Jesus. They must go because you have released from you heart those whom have hurt you, including yourself. It is so natural for us to hate someone who we know is deliberately trying to hurt us but the truth is that I had no resentment in my heart towards Miss Williams. As a matter of fact, I can truly say that I love her and really would love for her to find peace with God and with herself. My main concern is the condition of her soul and what will happen to her children as a result of her wickedness to the people of God.

I am grateful to God that He thought enough of me to allow me to go through so many challenges, heartaches and pain at the hands of Miss Williams and many others. God used Miss Williams to teach me to love and forgive even when I know that the person was deliberately trying to hurt me. As a result of that kind of heart I believe that I was spiritually elevated in my prayer life. I believe that I even prayed while I was sleeping. I know that I also worshipped in my sleep. There have been times when I turned in the middle of the night and I heard myself worshipping the Lord. I have also seen scriptures in my sleep. These are some of the things that kept me going in the heat of the various battles.

The battles were not only various but they were ongoing. One morning I woke up and I had the sniffles. I did not pay too much attention to it because I rarely have a cold and even when I did I knew it would quickly pass. That same afternoon I had an appointment with a prospective team member. This was one of those done deals and I was only going to her home for her to sign the agreement. During our conversation my nose kept running like a faucet. My nose was running so badly that I was somewhat embarrassed but I kept going. Needless to say, the person changed her mind for whatever reason. It was disappointing but this is normal in any business situation. People do change their mind.

That afternoon on my way home I stopped to get some over the counter medication for the runny nose which was really irritating me by this. Surprisingly, that did not work and I also realized that the tote bags that I normally carried over my shoulder I hardly had the strength to lift them anymore. My body became drained and weak but I kept going throughout the weekend and into Monday morning.

That week my new church which happened to be a Deliverance ministry was hosting a week of deliverance service. The guest speakers were Dr. Rebecca Brown author of "He came to Set the Captives Free" and her husband David. The second night of the service some sisters and myself were on our way home and I mentioned to them that I was not feeling too good and that I have this terrible cold. A sister recommended some home remedy that I tried. The next morning I felt a little better but I was still not feeling great.

A couple days after I was talking to a maintenance worker from the building that I lived in and he said to me that I sounded horrible. It was a few days after the runny nose had started and by this I could hear water gushing on my chest. He continued to say to me that recently he was feeling sick and when he went to the doctor he was told that two more days and he would have died. He said to me that I sounded worse than he did. I said to him that if by the end of the week I did not feel better I would go to the doctor. He had no idea about the warfare that I was experiencing in my life. By this I had already sensed that this was not normal sickness but it was another attack being launched by Miss Williams and her demonic imps.

I had a delivery to do that evening and because I was feeling so drained at the end of the day I went straight home. I had developed the reputation among my customers of not missing my appointments and to always be punctual. So I called my client the next day to apologize for not being able to meet with her the previous evening. She seemed a little concerned and she said "Sheron, that is not like you to miss your appointment what is going on?" This was a woman my senior who liked me and admired the way that I was vigilantly building my business so she was very supportive. In one of our previous conversations, for whatever reason, she had mentioned that she was of Cherokee descent. I remember looking in her eyes one day and said Dee if I did not know that you like me I would be very afraid of you. I said that because of what I felt when I looked into her eyes. She looked at me and smiled shaking her head as if to say "Sheron only you would be so bold and that is why I like you." She was a very sweet woman but not someone you would want to mess with.

So I started explaining to her that I was not feeling well and that was why I was calling to apologize and to reschedule her. She then asked "Sheron who is in your apartment with you?" I said I was alone." She said "Keep talking," which I did. She said to me that there was a woman in my apartment and she went on to describe my former roommate as if she had met the woman before. Dee had no idea what was going on because I had never discussed it with her. I did not want my clients to think I was weird so I never discussed my spiritual battles. I did not need to scare away my customers. I am very well aware of the fact that not everyone can or want to relate to this type of occurrence.

Dee asked me where did I drop my sword. I told her that I did not drop it. I began explaining to her that the only thing I can think of was that I do not fast frequently anymore because now that I was no longer in the same space with Miss Williams I wanted to nurture my body. Dee suggested that we pray. So I prayed out loud and when it was her turn she prayed silently. We talked for a while and then I hung up the phone.

After I hung up I decided to retire a little earlier than usual that night so I proceeded to get ready for bed. When I eventually got under the sheets I started to feel extremely hot like I was literally burning up. I began to pray and repeated the word of God. I prayed and repeated scriptures and apply the Blood of Jesus. I prayed and twisted and turned and prayed until after a few minutes I saw my roommate walked off my chest. I was still awake when this happened. When she walked off she paused briefly and shoved my right knee as if to say, "You got away again". I started pleading the Blood of Jesus against the spirit of

81

witchcraft. Immediately afterwards I could breathe without hearing the sound of water on my chest. The runny nose also stopped immediately. Bear in mind that Miss Williams is not dead she is a woman who is very much alive. As a matter of fact as I am writing this book she is a member of another church in Brooklyn. When she realized that she was defeated again she went to visit Dee at her home. Dee said that she dealt with Miss Williams' spirit her way. I was never led to ask.

WHO REDEEMETH THY LIFE FROM DESTRUCTION; WHO CROWNETH THEE WITH LOVINGKINDNESS AND TENDER MERCIES.

Psalm 103:4

CHAPTER SEVEN

PRESERVED BY GOD

When thou passest through the waters, I will be with thee; and through the rivers, they shall not overflow thee: when thou walkest through the fire, thou shalt not be burned: neither shall the flame kindle upon thee. Isaiah 43:2

I have relatives who live in Maryland and one brother in particular kept asking me to relocate. I resisted for quite a while not wanting to leave my church or the business I had built in New York. I had done enough relocating and I thought this was it. I was staying in New York. So I kept going about my merry way doing what I have been doing all along and that was to build my business in a city that never sleeps.

One late afternoon as I was on Wall Street hurrying to make deliveries I had an open vision. The Lord showed me myself in the pulpit at my brother's church in Maryland. I saw it but I kept going because the only thing on my mind at that time was to meet with my clients before the offices were closed. I strongly sensed that God was calling me into ministry but it is amazing how sometimes we want to call the shots by telling Him how and when. So many of us have learned the hard way that God's way is not our way and His thoughts are not our thoughts. I kept suppressing the call to go into ministry and the tug of the Holy Spirit to surrender. I really kept thinking that I needed more time.

We human beings are very interesting creatures. We were created by Almighty God and in John 1:3 it says "All things were made by him; and without him was not any thing made that was made." Yet we, mere dust, oftentimes want to dictate to a powerful God what is best for us. I kept saying to God when I become a Director or a National Sales Director then I would pursue ministry. I rationalized and even said to God I needed to be financially settled before I could do this. I rationalized my disobedience by saying to God that I was already in ministry because when I serve my clients they were always asking for prayers. I wanted to believe that doing my business was full time ministry because at almost every stop there was prayer, prayer requests or testimony.

I went to Queens one day to deliver perfume to a client who insisted that I prayed for her. She was a Christian whom God had healed of multiple sclerosis but because of her ungodly lifestyle she was back in the wheelchair. As she sat on the couch and I stood over her praying I saw the demons jumped from her trying to get to me but they were obviously blocked. I turned to her and I said "Valerie, listen up, you need to repent and go back to church so that you can be totally delivered."

Due to the list of excuses, I kept doing it my way until one day my whole life seemed to crumble around me. The next thing I knew I was asking my brothers to come help me relocate to Maryland. It was as if a whirlwind took me from New York to Maryland. When I got to Maryland I was so exhausted that I slept for two weeks like someone who was in a coma. After recuperating from exhaustion I was still looking back to those clients I had left in New York.

We hinder our blessings so many times by looking back to the place or situation that God had just delivered us from. All He is saying is that He has something better for us up ahead. I would service clients from different companies moving between floors on Wall Street delivering mostly preordered products. This was no easy task but I had a passion for my business.

However, God now wanted to channel that passion into winning more souls for His Kingdom. So, I kept traveling back and forth every month sometimes staying two to three weeks within a month to service my clients and to encourage my team. It was just so hard to let go of that customer base since Maryland was not as financially productive to me.

One day as I got off the bus in Brooklyn a lady came up to me and she called me by name. I answered with a bright smile thinking that she was a customer. She called my name and told me who she was. I immediately recognized the name as a friend of Miss Williams so I stood at a distance looking suspiciously at her. She said "No! No! We are no longer friends." She then asked me if I have ever met anybody as wicked as Miss Williams. She went on to tell me that Miss Williams did not seek outside help to do her evil but she was a major source and conduit of the evil she displayed. I told her that I was well aware of that fact, while still keeping my distance.

Minnie was a long time friend of Miss Williams because she had mentioned her name to me once or twice while we were roommates. She had known this woman for a while because they were coworkers many years ago in Jamaica. When I left Miss Williams invited her to come take my place and somehow convinced her that I was the wicked one. Minnie gladly accepted the offer thinking that her friend Miss Williams was the innocent party in all of this. She went on to tell me that she had been looking for me for three years. She even went to my old church looking for me and when she realized that I was no longer attending that congregation she said that her heart fell to the ground.

Minnie said one morning she was making cornmeal porridge and Miss Williams came over the stove and twiddle her fingers over the porridge. Minnie said her belly hurt her so badly that she felt as if she was going to die. She told me that she had never been so broke in her life. All her money had been drained and literally sucked away as if something devoured it. She said it was warfare after warfare and she tried so desperately to get out but it was extremely difficult.

She shared with me how she felt trapped because she could not seem to get away from all the attacks that were coming against her. Minnie said that it took her a long time to move because she could never come up with the moving cost. While she was speaking my heart went out to her because I knew what she had gone through. Feeling a bit more relaxed, I looked at Minnie and I could see the grace of God and the light of Christ in her. This confirmed to me that Miss Williams had an assignment from Satan to try and destroy Christians who were not playing church. My mission, at that point, became that of liberating the children of God from people like Miss Williams by sharing my story.

Isaiah 43: 1 – 2 said "But now thus said the Lord that created thee, O Jacob and he that formed thee, O Israel, Fear not: for I have redeemed thee, I have called thee by thy name; thou art mine. When thou passed through the waters, I will be with thee; and through the rivers they shall not overflow thee: when thou walkest through the fire, thou shalt not be burned; neither shall the flame kindle upon thee." God preserves His children from evil. There is no force on this earth, above this earth or under the sea that can overthrow the power of God. No demonic force can overpower the Blood of Jesus Christ. We have to believe that to be able to walk in total victory and overcome the attacks of the enemy. God loves His children so much that He allowed Minnie and I to run into each other, even though I was no longer living in New York. This was so that Minnie could get closure and I could get even more confirmation that this was nothing short of an assignment against the purpose of God on my life.

When you have been in intense warfare for as long as I have been usually your deliverance is a process. It also depends on all the different darts and arrows that were sent your way. You have to make sure that there is no residue left in your spirit or anything left in your home that is delaying your total breakthrough. You also get your deliverance when you have learnt to release the mental trauma of the experiences that you have been through.

When I had just relocated to Maryland my brother and I would attend a 6:00 am Wednesday morning intercessory prayer meeting in Washington DC. One morning as I got up and stood in the bathroom trying to stay awake I heard the words "Shut up". It was not loud so it did not fully register in my mind seeing that I was still drowsy. As I drove down the highway I heard the words again but this time it was in a commanding voice and much louder. "Shut up!" I immediately blurted out "Lord, I am not talking." When I responded it dawned on me that even though my mouth was not moving my mind was rehearsing the incidents I had experienced at a hundred miles per hour. The Lord wanted me to control my thoughts so that I would not be held hostage to the past as this would delay my total freedom. Even though I had changed my physical location I had to retrain my mind to learn to live without thinking constantly of being in danger. The experiences were traumatic to say the least.

It is similar to a soldier who has been in Afghanistan for years fighting in the war. When that soldier returns to the American soil his mind will have to be reprogrammed to living in a country where he does not have to walk down the street in military gear with weapons strapped on him all the time. As it is in the physical so it is in the spiritual. Some of us Believers have been on the frontline of the battle for a long time and so we think differently from those who have never been there.

In deliverance, at times, we have to change our position so that the Enemy cannot locate us easily and God knew that I needed to change state. This war went on for over a decade. I believe that God allowed it for a reason. He preserved me through the trials but it was now time for a new chapter. Now I had to learn how to process my experiences and also how to walk in wisdom with what I had learned. Now it was time for the manifestation of the demonstration of the power of God in my life on a different level.

" SPEAK TO YOUR ENEMIES TO DESTROY ONE ANOTHER"

Sheron M. Clarke

CHAPTER EIGHT

THE UNFOLDING OF GOD'S DIVINE PURPOSE

Jesus saith unto her, Said I not unto thee, that, if thou wouldest believe, thou shouldest see the glory of God? John 11:40

When I relocated to Maryland I was still spending a lot of time in New York and so the mental adjustment was not immediate. One day a sister in the business who lived in New York said to me that she has a church mother who would love to pray for me. She said she had shared with her some of what I had gone through while living in New York and she wanted to meet me.

Initially, I was feeling a bit apprehensive but I eventually went to see this mother of her church on one of my trips into New York. Her church was a non-denominational, evangelical church located in Brooklyn. Mother Moody welcomed me into her home and we talked a bit. Then she anointed me from the crown of my head to the soles of my feet and called upon God on my behalf. She said to me that they have buried my hair. She said "They took you to the graveyard so that when people look at you they don't see Sheron instead they would see death."

I knew she was speaking truth because there was a season in my life where I knew that I must have looked in the mirror to get dress everyday but I was not seeing my face or my beauty. When this veil of covering (as my Pastor refers to it) was broken that was when I realized that someone had covered me in the spirit. People who are evil do this to others to block their progress in life. These evil people do this for various reasons none of which is good. They can cover you financially so that it becomes very difficult for you to prosper, if ever at all. They can also cover you so that the opposite sex will not be attracted to you. They can cover you so that you will never get employed. You will go for interviews until you are blue in the face and no one will call you. To remove it you simply go to God by faith and ask Him to wash you in the Blood of Jesus Christ. You pray that any covering that has been placed over you, over your destiny, or over your star be removed in the Name of Jesus Christ.

Mother Moody cried on me as if I was her daughter. She told me that I should not just repeat the 91st Psalm casually but she wanted me to read it aloud and with authority. I bless God for servants who are authentic and have a heart for his people. I thank God for warriors of Jesus Christ who are willing to cry out on the behalf of the people of God when they need it most.

Down in my heart and based upon my experiences it was very clear to me and the people around me that God had a special calling for me and that this was mere preparation. After all, He does equip the called. The problem in the church is that some people run ahead of the call and at times without some form of preparation. This is why there is so much chaos in many churches.

When churches stress mainly the intellectual aspect of preparation then their ministers are theoretically ready, they have the degrees on the wall to prove it but they are spiritually inept. Then there are others who have a few spiritual experiences and they think they know it all. They have no formal, organized training so they operate as loose cannons so to speak. In either case the church members suffer. There need to be balance in that one is formally trained along with being thoroughly trained by the Holy Spirit. The Holy Spirit is the best Teacher. Seminary has nothing over the Holy Spirit but there need to be some theological training. Jesus told His disciples in John 14:26 "But the Comforter, which is the Holy Ghost, whom the Father will send in my name, he shall teach you all things, and bring all things to your remembrance, whatsoever I have said unto you." He is the most crucial part of our training.

In order for us to be powerful vessels unto God we also have to go through processes that will allow our hearts to be aligned with the heart of God so we can be usable. We have to be broken so that God can mold us and fashion us to be more like Him. If we do not know Him in a very intimate and real way, how will we tell others who God is and what He has delivered us from? David knew God in a way that pleases Him and because of his obedience to God in 1 Samuel 13:14 God said that David is a man after His own heart. God wants that kind of relationship with every one of His children. But like most physical family with children some will be obedient, some will be somewhat obedient and some might even dare to be rebellious. Every test, however, is to bring us closer to God.

In Psalm 31:1 David said "In thee, O lord, do I put my trust; let me never be ashamed: deliver me in thy righteousness." In verse 4 he says "Pull me out of the net that they have laid privily for me: for thou art my strength." The Enemy has a way of trying to take away your dignity. He will try to humiliate you and wear you down so that if you are not careful you will have no more will power to fight back. You cannot fight back in your own strength. We are not strong enough to fight the Enemy because remember that he has some power too. It is in the most troubling times of our lives that we really get to know God in a very personal way. If you have ever been humiliated and disgraced by the Enemy know that you are a prime candidate for greater anointing.

COURAGE UNDER FIRE!!

It was the Thanksgiving season so I went to the bank for cash to prepare for Thanksgiving only to find out that my account was inaccessible. In the pit of my stomach I knew that something was terribly wrong. After all, creditors had been calling and I was no longer working my business like I use to. Disheartened, I jumped in my car heading for home. It was cold, dark, and raining that evening as I headed for a major highway. I was so frustrated and emotionally tired that I was unable to find the right button to defog the windshield.

However, the bank situation just pushed me over the edge and I was spiritually broken. Through all the tests I had gone through, I had queried, I wondered, I talked to God and yes I cried but I had never lost it emotionally. I have the personality and the resolve in me to be able to bear a lot. Some people fall to pieces at the first sign of disaster. I see disaster and I have learnt over the years to say "Lord, let me see how you will deliver me out of this one." However, there have been so many challenges. Jesus said in Matthew 11:28 "Come unto me, all ye that labor and are heavy laden and I will give you rest." The tears were pouring from the depths of my spirit and I was emotionally distraught. I made a right turn into the nearest parking lot and cried out to Jesus. When I screamed His Name I literally saw Jesus in the spirit and it was as if He turned around when I screamed His Name. In Jeremiah 33:3 "He said call unto me, and I will answer thee, and shew thee great and mighty things, which thou knowest not."

I poured my heart out to Him. Even though the situation did not change immediately in the physical, I knew that God would take me through whatever lies ahead. With eyes closed I sat there meditating for a little while trying to gain composure before going back on the highway. When I felt a bit relieved I wiped my tears and happened to look around at my surroundings. When I looked up I was parked directly underneath a sign that read "High Point High School." I smiled and said to God "You have such a sense of humor".

For me this was the straw that broke the camels back. This was one of the lowest points in my life and here I was parked underneath a sign that reads "High Point". God has a way of cheering up His children and He knows just what each of us needs. It is also when we have been thoroughly broken and is at our lowest that God can use us mightily. David said in Psalm 51:17 that the sacrifices of God are a broken spirit: a broken and a contrite heart, O God thou wilt not despise.

I made it through Thanksgiving and that weekend when I went to church I worshipped God like I had never worshipped before. One of the tricks of the Enemy is to stop our worship to God by putting relational, physical, spiritual or financial stumbling blocks in our path. He thought he had me so cornered that there was no way I was going to go up in church, on the choir at that and worshipped God as if I had lost my mind.

Brothers and sisters if you have to wait for your breakthrough to worship God then you have missed it. We worship while we are going through the hardship. We worship God when the money is not adding up to pay the bills. We worship God when that child is heading down the path of destruction and is refusing to listen. This is worshipping by faith. Faith is the substance of things hoped for the evidence of things not seen according to Hebrews 11:1. If we can see it then it is not faith. We need to take a page out of Job's book that worshipped even when every material possession including his children were taken away. He asked his friends "Shall we receive good at his hand and not evil?" When we have this mindset we frustrate the Enemy. That is how it should be and not the Enemy frustrating us. We have the weapon.

Finally I had to do a thorough examination of the situation in order to preserve my body and so I started building in Maryland as oppose to trying to hold on to my customer base in New York. True prosperity will not come if you are walking in disobedience. You cannot outrun or outsmart God. Take it from me you will lose.

As I was leaving a business function one day an ordained minister who was also a director in the company asked me what was going on. I said to her "I don't know, it seems like I take one step forward then two steps backward". I told her it was such a struggle to get to the next level, which for me was directorship. She said "Sheron, why don't you take one day out of your busy schedule just to be locked away with God and seek His face?" She suggested that I do no business activity, no phone calls, just spend time alone with God.

I eventually took her suggestion and on Wednesdays I quietly waited before the Lord in prayer and fasting. Shortly afterwards I recruited a new team member who told me that her church has Wednesday intercessory prayer at noon. I went and immediately loved the host who is a true Worshipper and Intercessor.

Later on as I registered for Bible School I remember feeling such sense of peace that if I had died at that moment I knew I would be happy to meet my Lord and Savior. I was right where God wanted me to be. I felt at that moment that I had finally stepped into the purpose of God for my life. I remember thanking the Lord for this opportunity to be edified by qualified teachers. I was still so hungry for God that I could hardly wait to start classes.

The only way you will experience a certain level of anointing in your life is to be very hungry for God. I was at my brother's house in Laurel one day in mid May when he had a friend who was visiting along with his family. They had two sons with them and one son was so very, very hyperactive that my heart went out to the couple. I left Laurel and headed for Bowie to my other brother's home but on my way the spirit of compassion for this family was very overwhelming. I interceded for them while driving and I could not tell you how I got to Bowie. When I parked at his house my sister-in-law had just pulled up also and was about to enter the garage. As we stood in the garage and I was speaking to her I saw smoke coming out of my mouth. She looked at me very surprised and said "I am talking and smoke is not coming out of my mouth but it is coming out of yours and it is not even cold". I said to her "It is nothing to be alarmed about but I was in intense prayer on my way coming over here".

God has not changed. In Acts 2: 19 it reads "And I will shew wonders in heaven above, and signs in the earth beneath; blood, and fire, and vapour of smoke." In Joel 2:29-30 it says "And also upon the servants and upon the handmaids in those days will I pour out my spirit. And I will shew wonders in the heavens and in the earth, blood, and fire, and pillars of smoke." He is the same God yesterday, today and forever according to Hebrews 13:8. I firmly believe that signs, wonders and miracles are very much a part of our Christian walk today. We cannot restrict God because of our unbelief. He will simply find someone else who believes His word and is radical enough in his faith to be obedient, even if it does not make him popular.

COURAGE UNDER FIRE!!

A year into Bible School the call of God upon my life was becoming not only more intense but very frequent. I could tell time was running out in trying to delay. God was tired of hearing my excuses and this was it. It became very clear that I was sent on this earth to be a clear, loud and powerful voice for God. I did not have a choice. I dreamt one night that I stood at the front of a bus in Brooklyn asking the passengers if anybody knew how to get to Kadesh Barnea. I was very adamant in trying to get the information so I could go to this place. When I woke up I recognized the word from the scriptures. It is a place that the children of Israel got to before they entered the Promised Land. It was the boundary around the Promised Land. See Numbers 34:1-4 and Joshua 10:41. About a week after that dream in my sleep one night I saw the words "How beautiful are the feet of them that bring good news" the biblical references that came to mind are Romans 10:15 and Isaiah 52:7.

I started getting academically prepared for what I knew and finally acknowledged as God's calling upon my life. I enjoyed my classes because the courses were thorough. My first year was fairly smooth. Peace in the classroom came to a screeching halt, however, when character and personalities started competing for attention. It was as if the Enemy said "Oh no you are getting too close to your purpose I have to try and stop you again.

In my second year the Director of the school appointed me as the class monitor. I knew this was not going to be easy but I was ready for the challenge. It was clear that the Enemy had raised its ugly head once again and if I did not accept this position then my training would have taken longer than was necessary. I felt like I was going to the war in Iraq on class nights. Spirits were manifesting like crazy. The spirit of anger, contention, strife, sabotage, cheating just to name a few, were very strong. Not only were they manifesting, it was obvious that somehow I was the target. When the spiritual attacks did not work there were strong physical confrontation. There were manifestations at almost every class. It brought back memories and I was feeling tense in the classes.

I had a dream one night where I saw myself in the bush somewhere in Africa. I stood between the trees and I saw some of my classmates lead by a senior year student entering a tree house. It was night but when I looked on the ground beside me I saw a skeleton in the bushes. When I woke up I asked the Lord to protect and cover me. I knew that the Enemy was stirring up my classmates against me in order to get me distracted and frustrated so I would not be able to finish my course.

As the call of God on my life got stronger I also noticed that my passion for my business was waning. I sell some products here and there but the fire for it was gone. So I was in school with no real income. One day a classmate purchased some items from me and so I delivered them to her. When she eventually paid me the check came back "insufficient funds". We were on holiday so I left a message on her voice mail telling her that the check came back but not to worry she could bring the cash when school reopens.

About two nights after this message was left on her phone I dreamt that my phone rang. In the dream I answered the phone then I asked the person to wait a little while I turned down the volume on my radio. After turning down the volume I picked up the receiver and greeted the person at the other end of the line. The voice on the other end was my classmate who had purchased the products. She was shouting and screaming in a horrible rage. She was screaming and asking me who dare me to call her house talking about a check. In the dream her hand came through the phone as if to rip my right ear off my head. It was so real that it frightened me out of my sleep. It was so scary that I heard myself screamed as I awoke. I lie in bed praying when I heard the voice of the Lord said to me "You can't lie down and fight. Get up!" I jumped up and started praying against every evil force, every arrow and every fiery dart that was sent toward me from this person, in Jesus' Name.

I knew that I was where God wanted me to be and I was obviously getting closer to my purpose and destiny in God. I believe that was why these demonic events started happening again with such intensity. One night I dreamt that I saw a huge imprint of Africa in the sky like a giant map and it was on fire. In the dream a friend was standing beside me and I kept pointing to the sky. I said "Look, Africa is on fire". I asked her if she could see it and she said she could not. I knew that God had a message in this for me but I had to wait for the unfolding of this particular vision.

The Lord speaks to me a lot through dreams and visions and I will never substitute this for His word. I believe that the Bible is the authoritative word of God. When I dream and get visions what I usually look for is how it lines up with the word, the nature and the will of God. If it is a prophetic dream it should manifest somehow, there must be confirmation.

When Intercessors get dreams from the Lord it is because He wants you to pray against that event or impending danger in someone's life. It does not always have to be about danger we also get pleasant dreams as well but of course, it is all up to God. Sometimes I will feel extremely drained and I know that I need to go kneel beside my bed or lie down and be still before God. Usually I will dose off for a bit and then he will reveal certain things to me. It can either be something that is about to happen or it could be something that will take place in another year or so. The Spirit of the Lord would warn me of impending danger in my life, for a family member, a friend or total stranger whom I will probably never meet on earth. My task is to intercede for those people.

In 2003 I started having visions where I was seeing the death of one of my brothers. Almost every other month I would see him either dying or already in the casket. At one of our Wednesday noonday Intercessory Prayer meeting I asked for prayer because I kept asking the Lord if it was a spiritual death or a physical death. Spiritual death is just as bad as physical death but in my heart I knew that he was in grave (no pun intended) danger. In one of the visions I saw him in a sky blue shirt lying in the casket. While he was laying there his daughter who was about seven at the time came near the casket, looked down on him and then looked over at me.

During this time I was constantly on three- day dry fasts seeking the Lord on this matter and crying out for mercy on his behalf. On one of these fasts he happened to come by the house and I was locked away in my bedroom. I remember him going down the stairs and complaining to the family that I needed to eat. He said she is always locked up in the room praying. Little did he know that this one was specifically on his behalf.

In October of 2004 I was on a retreat and I got another one of these soul wrenching visions. In this vision I saw a skeleton on the ground, its bones were white of course but it was also covered in blood. When I woke up I felt sick to my stomach and could not enjoy the fellowship anymore. My spirit was so troubled I even asked God why do I have to be getting these kinds of visions. I tried to make the best of the occasion but I left the resort burdened.

COURAGE UNDER FIRE!!

A week after I got home from the retreat I got a phone call from a sister who was also in the cosmetic business. She was calling from Kansas because she got my name from another sister who told her that I would pray for her. After speaking with her for a little our spirits connected and so I stopped what I was doing and knelt in prayer with her. As I got off my knees the phone rang and it was my sister-in-law calling to say that my brother was just in a motorcycle accident and he was rushed to the hospital. My other brother and I drove together to the hospital but on our way, my face was set like a flint in the spirit so we hardly exchanged a word. When I saw Glen the bones in his face were broken, nose broken, jaw broken, he could not breathe properly and he had lost a lot of blood. He looked so badly beaten up that at age 35 they labeled him as a 56 year old male.

It was a Friday night, so they examined the extent of his injuries and tried to stabilize him. I was speaking to his attending nurse and she mentioned how many of these accidents she has seen and how lucky my brother was to be alive. This had nothing to do with luck it had been an ongoing battle in the spirit realm for the last year at least. Only God could have kept him because when he got hit off his motorcycle what he remembered was his spirit leaving his body. He even mentioned afterwards that he had seen our aunt who was dead, my cousin Cislyn's mother. At the approximate time of the accident I was on my knees having prayer with Cari whom I had never met. I could easily have told her to let us pray at another time because I was about to make some business calls. However, God would have it that after He has been showing me such vivid visions of what could have been Glen's death for a year, that at the precise time of the accident, I was on my knees praying. Who but God? There is none like Him. God gets all the glory in this.

With pain racking his body we were eventually told that on Monday morning the doctor would perform a tracheotomy on him so that he could breathe easily. On Monday afternoon I went and picked up his now eight year old daughter from school before going to the hospital. By the time we got there he was out of surgery and back in the intensive care unit. As we approached the bed I noticed that he was wearing a plain, sky blue hospital gown, his eyes were closed, the tube was in his throat, his jaws were wired shut and he was very still. My niece walked over to the other side of the bed to stand beside her mother, she looked down in her father's face and then looked over at me. It was then that the dream came back to my mind and I almost screamed in the ICU. It was just too much for my mortal body to deal with.

All I kept saying was "Oh my God! Oh my God! Oh my God! I get so many visions and dreams that I have to journal to keep up. Eventually, I mentioned to him what had been happening since 2003 and how I had shared it with some of my prayer partners. I refuse to take God's glory. These are just a few of the visions and dreams that God gave me that I have used as examples in this book to show the awesomeness of our God. My prayer has always been that he would realize how special he is to God and that he would totally surrender his heart to Him.

When the Lord has called you as an Intercessor to stand in the gap for his people it is expected that the Enemy will try to retaliate somehow. One afternoon in the middle of 2005 I was about to leave the house to do some business but when I got to the front door I felt very drained. I was so drained that I went back upstairs to kneel at my bedside to gather myself. While kneeling I dosed off and I had a vision. I saw myself in my car at the intersection near my home. In the vision I was approaching a major intersection close to my home but the car would not stop. I kept pumping the brake but to no avail. When I woke up I cried unto the Lord to cancel any accident and death that the Enemy has orchestrated in hell for me or for anyone that I know. When I get these visions I do not worry about it because I believe that once I pray I must trust that He is well able to take care of me. I have learnt to pray according to what God has shown me and lay it at His feet

We had a ceremony at our school and Bishop Harry Jackson, Pastor of Hope Christian Center was our guest speaker. After delivering his message he spoke prophetically over some of my classmates and he pointed at me and said "Wipe your tears, God has heard your cry in the midnight hours. I see you in the third world before thousands preaching the gospel."

I knew I was called but up to this point I still had not gone to my Pastor to share with him that I wanted to answer the call of God upon my life. However, I was preparing myself even before I spoke to my leader. So, in November 2005 I eventually went to my Pastor to let him know that I was answering my call into the ministry. He graciously agreed and the process of training in the church also began. I do not believe in doing anything halfheartedly. I believe in compassion, conviction, loyalty and timing and that was why I waited. Not only did I want to be sure beyond the shadow of a doubt that God had called me but also that the timing was right. Somewhere in there was a little fear of the unknown mixed in as well. However, the Holy Spirit had trained me over the years that it was not only good to know that I was called but I needed to be sensitive to God's timing.

I had observed enough people in ministry who were not sure if they were really called or they knew they were called but they were not sure what area they were called to serve in. Or they felt out of sync because they had run ahead of God. God knows me and I know myself well enough to know that if there were any doubt in my mind about my call I could not be effective in ministry and therefore I would not have stayed.

In October 2006 at about 8:00 am I was on my way to work driving down I-95 listening to my worship music and having a wonderful time in the Lord. As I turned on the exit ramp going onto 495 I heard a very faint knock on my car. The next thing I knew the car was careening off the highway heading for the bushes and shrubs to my left. I kept pressing the brake but to no avail. I was so shocked while this was happening that I was asking the Lord if I was really having an accident. I made a sharp right turn to try to get the car to stop and it ended up wrapping around a utility pole. The car was totaled but thank God I walked away unhurt. There were no broken bones and neither did I feel any pain. This was nothing short of a miracle.

Two days later we were at the place where the car was towed and an employee asked us who was the person that was in the car. I looked at him and said I was. He looked at me and he was in shock. I said "I know, only God could have kept me". At about 6:00 am on the morning of the accident my cousin Dawnette, who lives in England and who was attending a seminar in North Carolina, was praying fervently against the spirit of death. When she heard about the accident we were just praising God for His hand of mercy toward me one more time.

By this I had completed my Biblical Studies and two days after the accident I was scheduled to graduate from Chesapeake Bible College. I walked across stage pain free to receive my degree in Christian Ministry and I bless God that I am more than conqueror through him that loves me. I, too, like the children of Israel who watched the Egyptians drowned in the Red Sea can also sing "Who is like unto thee, O Lord, amongst the gods?

COURAGE UNDER FIRE!!

Who is like thee, glorious in holiness, fearful in praises doing wonders?" Exodus 15:11.

"IF THE CATERPILLAR DOES NOT STRUGGLE HOW WILL IT BECOME THAT BEAUTIFUL BUTTERFLY WITH STRONG WINGS? SO MUST WE ALSO STRUGGLE AMIDST ADVERSITIES TO BE ABLE TO SOAR"

Sheron M. Clarke

CHAPTER NINE

THE ULTIMATE CALL

So the last shall be first and the first shall be last: for many are called, but few chosen. Matthew 20:16

On December 2, 2007 I went before the congregation to preach my initial sermon where I was officially licensed before God and man to preach the gospel of Jesus Christ. What a journey! Was everyone thrilled? Absolutely not. To be honest with you I was hoping that now that I was officially a minister of the gospel I would get some rest. After all, we are all called to run this race and to fight this battle together for the Lord. I believe we are all serving the same God and we have one common Enemy. What could be so hard to comprehend in this whole scenario?

Something apparently happened, however, in the spirit realm the night that I delivered my initial sermon. It seemed like it was the beginning of spiritual warfare in the pulpit. The saying is new level new devil. This was another eye opener for me. Somehow, I still wanted to believe, after all I have been through, I really wanted to believe that it was going to be smoother now that I was in leadership and we were all together in ministry. After all we should have one common goal and that should be to annihilate the Enemy. I was ready!

Instead I saw cliques being formed against me. I experienced the spirit of sabotage against the ministry that I was appointed to lead by the same people who appointed me. How can one think it is right to appoint someone to lead a ministry then turn around and sabotage the Lord's work so that the person would look bad or fail?

This was nothing but the spirit of insecurity and competition that is sickening in the house of the Lord and has nothing to do with our God. I Peter 5:8 states "Be sober, be vigilant; because your adversary the devil, as a roaring lion, walketh about, seeking whom he may devour." Anyone the Enemy can use to sabotage the plan of God he will, even if they are in the house of God. Is there any wonder why we do not experience the healings and deliverance on the magnitude that the apostles of old did? Is there any wonder that we have lost our savor and the world has little respect for us?

I refused to move out of the will of God because of struggles. So I did all that God required of me where I was planted. I believe in being faithful no matter what the obstacles until the assignment is completed. During my time at this church among other duties I served as Lay Pastor for the Evangelism Ministry for two years and started a vibrant Nursing Home Ministry that I left in their care.

I love to serve outside of the four walls so I am not one of those ministers who get depressed if I am not allowed to serve in the pulpit. I get a thrill and such joy in my heart when I share the gospel in prisons, nursing homes, on the street, in the marketplace, anywhere outside where there is a need and there is always a need. They realized after a while that they could not spite me with their ungodly way of conducting ministry. I was not looking to build an empire in the pulpit instead my ministry was outside. That was what God was equipping me for by allowing me to go through all those warfare and that was why the Enemy had been fighting so fiercely. I diligently served in this ministry for eight years working and waiting on the direction of God.

One day while sitting at my desk at work I heard the spirit of the Lord said "You are released." When I tendered my resignation the Pastor was so angry that he stated that he was revoking my ministerial license. His reason was that I did not have any direction in ministry. I wrote him a sincere thank you letter of about a page and a half outlining the list of assignments that were accomplished while I was at his church and a list of what I was currently doing. I had learnt a long time ago to be grateful to folks for the good they have done even if they eventually turned against you. I always remember the good over the bad so I continued to keep my eyes on Jesus and walk in obedience to my Lord and Savior. At the end of the journey He is the One I will have to stand before and give an account to for the things that I have done.

Over the years of going through intense warfare God had trained my spiritual ears to hear Him over man's ego and pride. Even though I heard the voice of God clearly, being human, I was still examining and reexamining everything that took place. The Enemy and my flesh kept reminding me that I was not even at the first level in ministry now that he had "revoked" my license. I knew in my heart that spiritually I was well beyond where men wanted to keep me but it was a fight for it to manifest in the earth realm. Then one day the Lord spoke to me while I was in my home and He asked me, "Title or crown?" I answered "Crown Lord." That was when I got closure in my heart concerning their behavior. My reward is not from man but from God and I needed to be reminded.

I know thy works: behold I have set before thee an open door and no man can shut it: for thou hast a little strength, and hast kept my word, and has not denied my name according to Revelation 3:8. One day as I was doing my dishes and thinking about Him I heard a small voice that clearly said "Ministry

Without Walls." The voice was so calm and still that it took a few seconds for it to register in my mind what I had just heard. It was still but the words were instantly engraved upon my heart.

I repeated the words Ministry Without Walls and it was as if I heard it a second time. I continued my daily tasks but the Spirit of God had made an impartation in my spirit and it was about to be manifested in the earth. God had placed in my spirit almost fifteen years ago that He wanted me to lead a prayer ministry. The group of women, all dressed in full white, kneeling with their head to the ground, that the Lord had shown me almost 15 years prior was a glimpse of where He wanted to take me.

This vision was shown to me at a time in my life when everything around me was shaking. The storms were raging left, right and center. It was constant spiritual attack one after another but God will give His children glimpses of where He wants to take us in order to encourage us through the battles. We have to go through the battles because this is our only method of preparation. James 1:2-3 says "Brethren count it all joy when we fall into divers temptations; knowing this, that the trying of your faith worketh patience. But let patience have her perfect work, that ye may be perfect and entire, wanting nothing."

When I was passing through several waves of warfare and persecution the Lord reminded me of His purpose for me by showing me this group of women in full white. After a while I knew that the time for its manifestation was drawing close but it was still not quite time. During this time I never became anxious by bothering God and constantly asking Him how, when or questioning His wisdom. I kept serving in the churches that He placed me. I firmly believe that anywhere a child of God enters or serves that place should be better for it after he/she has left. They should know that a true child of God passed through. You should not be the instigator of turmoil as you move to the next assignment. That is not of God and it will damage your ministry and most of all taint the anointing. Treat others well and treat your leaders well, even if they do not like you. You should still show love and obediently serve until the Lord tells you to move on and when He does you do so with grace and in peace. I humbly served while crying out to God for more of His grace and more of Him. I have had an insatiable hunger for God that has been unquenchable over the years and I pray to God that I will always have this desire for Him.

So many situations have come upon me to try and quench this hunger and thirst for God. But what I have discovered in my journey is that if we do not faint in the midst of adversity, God will elevate us in the spiritual realm to another level. Our faith will increase, the anointing will increase and you will be so much closer to God. God is not trying to be unkind or to cause us harm by allowing these challenges. He wants our heart. God wants to know that when we are promoted He can trust us with His gifts and anointing. He wants us to know who we are in Him so that we will stand in the midst of any trial. When we are walking in our calling He wants us not to forget why we were promoted in the first place. He does not want us to steal His glory when He is using us. He wants to know that our heart is so in line with His heart that we will have compassion for His people.

He molds us so that we will have a heart for those who are lost and on their way to hell. He fashions us so that we will have a heart for a mother who has to decide which one of her children she should give the rice and beans to today. He wants us to have a heart for that man or woman or child who has come to the end of their rope and has lost hope in their future. Some people are lost because their spiritual compass has been broken and it needs fixing. We have the answer and it is Jesus Christ. We are not called so that we can brag about our big houses, latest model cars, children, spouse, our material possessions or even our spiritual gifts. We are called with one message and that is to tell others about the hope that lies in our having a relationship with Jesus Christ. Simply put Jesus says in John 14: 6 "I am the way, the truth, and the life: no man cometh unto the Father, but by me." Tell your story of what Jesus Christ has done for you.

It is so important that we learn to discern our season. Timing is everything when we are vessels in the hand of God. He is the One that needs to open the door – not us. He is the One who knows exactly when we are spiritually and emotionally ready. If we are too late we will miss the mighty move of God. If we get out of the furnace too soon then we become half-baked and unpalatable. We need to be just right for the Master's use. Prepared at the right temperature and for the precise length of time.

When God breathed the words Ministry Without Walls into my spirit I shared what had happened to a group of friends that I was already praying with. They were so excited that immediately we all knew that it was the beginning of a new era in our prayer lives. The Lord led me to officially start Ministry Without Walls in August 2008. Also in 2008 Haiti had experienced four hurricanes within the season and so God laid it upon our hearts to bless this nation. This was the beginning of our outreach ministry. In February 2009 we started our first evangelical outreach on Finns Lane in Maryland where we held services the last Friday of each month until August of that year.

Prayer requests were coming from all over the United States and outside of the country as well with people needing healing from all types of cancer, other illnesses, demonic oppression, relational and financial issues. We bless God for the miracles that came forth as a result of His faithfulness toward His people. In II Chronicles 7:14 it says "If my people, which are called by my name, shall humble themselves, and pray, and seek my face, and turn from their wicked ways; then will I hear from heaven, and will forgive their sin, and will heal their land."

Not only has God directed us to stand in the gap for the nations but to also bless them in a tangible way through our finances. Ministry Without Walls was led of the Lord to align with ministries that are on the frontline for the Lord. These ministries shelter the homeless, they provide food for the poor, protect the persecuted and take care of the spouses of martyrs. They also provide reading materials and essential items to the underground church. They distribute Bibles and other literatures to help Muslim Background Believers in their newly found faith. Radios tuned to the gospel are also distributed in remote areas in countries like Vietnam, Indonesia, Mongolia to name a few. We also provide Sunday morning church services every two weeks at Genesis Health Care formerly known as Sligo Creek Nursing Home and Rehabilitation Center located in Maryland.

God has been steadily sending those whom He has chosen to be a part of this ministry and as a result of which we are growing. The Lord recently added male intercessors who are faithful and who love the Lord. One of the reasons why this ministry is such a ground for miracles is that God is the one leading this prayer ministry and whatever He wants that is what we do. We have all suffered through various challenges in order to get to this place in our walk. Sis Joan McKenzie Bellillle whom I met in the cosmetic business is one such person. While pregnant with her third child the doctor told her to write her will because of blood clot that was found in her lungs. She changed her doctor, called upon God then went on to have her fourth child. That was nine years ago. We are talking about radical faith. Sis Sheila McNabb along with three other members of the prayer team were women I had the privilege of meeting while actively building my cosmetic business. Sis Pauline Barrett whom I met at the bank so many years ago has recently given her life to the Lord and is now a member of the prayer team. Sis Lllly White my friend from Miami is a woman on fire for God who is also a member of Ministry Without Walls. These women I have known for at least fifteen years. Only God could have put together such complex puzzle in the midst of various battles and turmoil. I thank Him so much for the courage that He has forged out of me during such hardship. What is more amazing to me is that He gave me nerves of steel to be able to keep it together so that I could build wonderful relationships in the midst of deep adversity. I give God all the credit because it is definitely supernatural.

We are totally led by the Holy Spirit and our ministry scripture is Matthew 25: 35-36 which says "I was an hungred, and ye gave me meat: I was thirsty, and ye gave me drink: I was a stranger, and ye took me in: Naked, and ye clothed me: I was sick, and ye visited me: I was in prison, and ye came unto me." To be able to accomplish this task we walk in Psalm 133:1 "How good and how pleasant it is for brethren to dwell together in unity."

I have a word of caution to ministries and especially Intercessors. When God assigns you to be the watchman there must be love and unity for the anointing of God to flow. Intercessory ministries should not be gossip centers neither should the members be backbiting or backstabbing each other and call it prayer requests. As a ministry we treat each person's request with confidentiality. We not only take requests and promise to pray for them but we actually do our best to get to everyone. It is work but we believe in following up. By following up on the persons asking for prayers we are able to see how they are doing and then pray intelligently and strategically for their total healing and deliverance, if necessary.

We are not into the fanfare of seeking men's applause for what God is doing. We give all the glory to Him. One morning as I was driving to work the Spirit of the Lord said to me that we are the Navy Seals of Intercessors. Our operation is to go in, do the job and move out without being seen while giving God all the glory for a job well done.

We are an ordinary group of women and men that God has molded and fashioned for such a time as this. We brag about our Lord and Savior Jesus Christ in Whom is all wisdom and knowledge. We can do nothing apart from Him. He is the One who directs our steps. He carries us on eagle's wings. He protects us from every trap of the Enemy. He is our Savior. He is our Deliverer. He is our Refuge. He is our Fortress. He is our Strong Tower. He is our Rock, our Shield and our Buckler. He is the I AM THAT I AM so whatever we need He is all that to us and more. We lack nothing in God. He is our Sufficiency, the Almighty God is He.

One night while we were having our prayer session I felt the urge to take out my robe and hang it where I could see it all the time. As a result of the behavior I had encountered I had placed my robe at the back of my outside closet. I often told friends and intercessors, however, that my ears are positioned at the mouth of God, so to speak. I needed to hear from God exactly what He was saying to me and what my next move was going to be.

I sat under the teaching and preaching of the AME Church Organization so that the word of God could bathe the wounds I had endured at my former church. Having a servant's heart, after six months I became a member and served as a lay leader for one year. Then the Lord led me to a newly formed non-denominational church where He obviously wanted me to observe how to build a ministry from scratch among other lessons.

Spiritually and technically I do not believe one can revoke one's license unless it was violated before God and man and that was not the case here. However, because it was spoken over me I needed to spiritually break that curse so that it would not follow me in ministry. I revoked the curse spiritually and physically went through the process again in 2011 at another church. So many people are walking around with spiritual arrows and darts attached to them because of curses that were spoken against them. In some cases sadly these were curses that were spoken against them even before they were born. God knew, of course, that these were some of the battles that I would be coming up against and that was why my preparation was so intense.

As I sat in the pulpit one Sunday morning I looked down on the program that I held in my hand and my eyes were drawn to the names of the ministerial staff listed on the back. It was as if the Enemy wanted me to feel insecure about myself sitting amongst my brothers and sisters who had a list of letters behind their names. Immediately the Spirit of the Lord jerked me back to reality and away from the spirit of intimidation and I heard Sheron "Miracle" Clarke. My middle initial starts with the letter M. I told the Lord thanks and a smile broke out in my spirit. It was a miracle that I had made it this far considering all that I had endured. So the Lord was reminding me that it was not about the degrees it was about Him.

I love the house of God because Jesus said in Matthew 16:18b "I will build my church; and the gates of hell cannot prevail." One of the things I said as a backslider was that whenever I get back in the church it was going to be one hundred percent, not ninety nine and a half. I believe that whatever I am doing it should be with passion. So I was not coming to church to play, this is not Sesame Street. When a witch can evangelize you by inviting you to the house of God, then tried to annihilate you in the process, you cannot play with the call of God upon your life. Believers need to be on high alert because Satan is not playing with us, in case we have not noticed.

We, as Intercessors are seeing quite a bit of requests from people whose bodies are under such spiritual attack that they can literally feel snakes, lizards, sharp arrows and crawlings all over them tormenting them day and night. Psalm 144:1 says "Blessed be the Lord my strength, which teacheth my hands to war and my fingers to fight." We need to be prepared to do warfare but I have one word of caution. Be sure that you are walking in holiness. This is one of our many greatest weapons. We cannot be living in sin or any type of compromise and think we can cast out demons. You are only fooling some church folks who do not have the spirit of discernment and you are also fooling yourself.

I really thank God for all my enemies who have taught me to do warfare. Without them I would not be qualified to lead such a powerful ministry as this. Ministry Without Walls International Inc. became a nonprofit organization in 2009 and we continue to be a blessing to the nations. I believe that what we have seen so far is just a tip of what God is about to do through us individually and collectively. I diligently served my church home while building Ministry Without Walls International, Inc and there is no greater joy to me than to be doing this. God rewards faithfulness and so when one assignment is completed He will direct us to the next.

Power of the Highest International Ministries is my current church home and my Pastor is Dorothy Nanga Lartey. A Prophetess for our time, a woman who is not afraid to go into the dark world to deliver the people of God. She reminds me of Deborah in Judges 4:9 when she said, "I will surely go with thee: notwithstanding the journey that thou takest shall not be for thine honour; for the Lord shall sell Sisera into the hand of a woman. And Deborah arose and went with Barak to Kedesh." She not only recognizes anointing but she is not afraid to embrace and encourage growth in her ministers. As a result of which God chose her to ordain me. With the journey I have had is it a coincidence that God has led me to an Apostolic and Prophetic African ministry? When I see how God is putting the puzzle of my life together He makes me smile in wonderment at His greatness.

It dawned on me a couple years ago that the Lord allowed me to sit and serve in different denominations as further training for what He wanted to do through me. Looking at my journey from New York until now it totally amazes me how God had orchestrated my life and lead me through all the spiritual land mines and rocky terrain. God has spared my life for me to tell the Body of Christ and the lost that no matter what you are going through, no matter how difficult the situation, there is absolutely no problem that God cannot see you through.

Salvation is free but the anointing is costly. There is a price to be paid for the anointing of God upon your life but it is so worth it. A lot of Christians want the anointing of God upon their lives without paying the price but it does not work that way.

COURAGE UNDER FIRE!!

God has to purge some hatred out of some of us. He has to purge resentment, lies, addictions, bitterness, unforgiveness, backbiting, pride, self- righteousness and witchcraft. These are just a few of the vices that must go. They have to be pressed out of us like grapes being pressed to make fine wine. Some of us are so stubborn that we have to stay a little longer on the press than others. However, we cannot fight with God. Struggling only makes it much harder and wastes a lot of time. We have our own agendas and preconceived notion as to what we think God requires of us. We cannot dictate to God. He is our Maker He knows exactly what He has programmed in our DNA and why He has placed us on the earth. Sometimes He merely whispers but we are too busy to hear so we keep going down the wrong path. He will get our attention somehow, one way or another.

So many Christians are restless because they are off course concerning their purpose. You cannot fit a square block into a circle and so many people are trying to do just that. Instead of learning to seek the face of God they do what they think other people expect of them. They do what society expects of them, what the church expects of them or what their parents expect of them instead of seeking God's will.

How do we really hear what God is saying? We hear from God through His word, through prayer and meditation. Jesus always took time to be alone with His Father. If He being divine needed to spend time with His heavenly Father while He was on earth, how much more should we mere mortals need to follow suit? We need to spend time with our heavenly Father getting to know Him. Instead of seeking only His hand we need to seek His face. In Psalm 103:7 it says "He made known his ways unto Moses, his acts unto the children of Israel." It is through knowing God that we really get to know who we are. We become His reflection, through his word and obeying Him. He will mirror to us who we are through His word. He will make our crooked path straight. Isaiah 45:2.

It does not mean that we will never make mistakes or even mess up every now and then but we will have a peace that passes all understanding because we are in his will. We are on the right path and His Spirit will bear witness with our spirit. When we are on purpose we have a fire in our soul. We become passionate for the things of God. We will do whatever God calls us to do even for free. Nothing can stop us. We have extra energy and we know it is supernaturally coming from God because it is not humanly possible. This kind of passion can only be borne out of adversity.

After we have been through these tests and trials when we emerge we will realize that we have a much closer walk with God. We bond with Jesus so to speak in the heat of adversity. When we are in love with God we learn to love ourselves, thereby learning to love others. We become more Christ like. Some people become bitter when they go through adversity but the way I look at it is if I am mad at God, if I declare God as my enemy then whom can I trust? Who will fight my battles? He is the only One who is faithful, He is the only One who is just. He is the only One who is loving and can forgive my sins. Who else can I turn to?

"DIVINATION MIXED WITH JESUS IS NOT JESUS CHRIST"

Sheron M. Clarke

CHAPTER TEN

NEVER MIX HIM!

You shall not eat anything with the blood, nor shall you practice divination or soothsaying. Leviticus 19:26

We serve a mighty God. Our God is All Powerful, He is Sovereign and He is our Deliverer. God sent His only begotten Son, Jesus the Christ to shed His blood on the cross so that we would not be slaves to Satan's wicked devices. Anything that comes against us as His children all we have to do is call upon His Name. All we have to do, if we have accepted Jesus Christ as Lord and Savior of our lives, is to apply the Blood of Jesus Christ to whatever situation that will come upon us.

We apply the Blood of Jesus to the situation by saying words like I cover my finances with the Blood of Jesus Christ. I soak my family in the Blood of Jesus Christ. We speak it by faith because God requires us to speak life into our circumstances and against strongholds. In the book of Genesis when God stepped out in the universe all He did was speak into the atmosphere and everything manifested. The day, the night, the sun, the moon, the stars, the animals were spoken into physical existence.
As Believers we need to use the word of God to apply to every situation in our lives and know that it is a faith walk. Habakkuk 2: 4 says "….the just shall live by faith." That is what God requires of us.

The problem is that when we go to God with our challenges and we do not get the answer when we want it, a lot of times we take matters into our own hands. Too many of us are quick to sell out Christ when we are faced with difficult situations. I have met quite a few Christians who have opened the door to satanic attacks by mixing Christ with New Age, Necromancy, Voodoo and others. I do not care how they call it doing it for "good luck." It is calling familiar spirits into your lives and telling Jesus Christ that you can handle this but He is incapable.

What we are doing when we go to the soothsayers is to tell Jesus Christ that the shedding of His Blood is not powerful enough. What we are saying is that we have more faith in satanic rituals, ceremonies, customs and traditions, and friends' ungodly advise than the word of the true and living God. What we are also saying is that God is powerful enough to blow breath into mankind but not strong enough to take care of our sicknesses, diseases, demonic attacks or financial turmoil.

Psalm 20:7 says " Some trust in chariots, and some in horses but we will remember the name of the Lord our God." We either trust God or we don't. We cannot mix unbelief with faith and think that God will move on our behalf. We cannot mix Jesus Christ with high society science and call it God. We cannot mix Jesus Christ with divination and think that God is pleased. If that is the case my brothers and sisters you have been deceived by the Enemy. He is laughing at you because your hands are dirty before God. Who shall ascend into the hill of the Lord? Or who shall stand in his holy place? He that hath clean hands and a pure heart; who hath not lifted up his soul unto vanity, nor sworn deceitfully that is Psalm 24:3-4.

Through all my warfare experiences I never used or relied on anything but the word of God and the Blood of Jesus Christ to deliver me. It was not even a thought. It is bad enough when someone who is still in darkness goes to see the soothsayer or the medicine man to solve his or her problems. However, what is unthinkable to me is that someone who claims to be a Believer of the Lord Jesus Christ would seek help from Satan. Why would you go to the Enemy's camp for help?

It is like two sets of family having a vicious feud and a child of one of the families fighting decides to go next door to ask for a plate of food. Do you see how absurd that would be? Then why do we go to the Enemy's camp to get help when our God is All Powerful? Where I am from that child would be thoroughly disciplined.

Once this spiritual door has been opened by us the Enemy has all legal right to inflict suffering, pain and even death on us because we have mingled with the unclean. We have relinquished our authority to him which Jesus Christ himself gave us in Luke 10:18 - 19 And he said unto them, "I beheld Satan as lightning fall from heaven. Behold, I give unto you power to tread on serpents and scorpions, and over all the power of the enemy and nothing shall by any means hurt you."

We whine and complain about the fact that Adam and Eve gave up their authority and privilege to the Enemy in the Garden of Eden. We fuss over the fact that we have so many trials and tribulations as a result of their disobedience and yet today we repeat the same sin - disobedience. We allow the Enemy to come into our homes and steal our kids, steal our spouses, steal our goods and money. He also steal our health and then we blame Adam and Eve saying if only they had not sinned back then we would not have to be going through all this.

Wake up people! Jesus Christ arose a victor from the tomb and because He rose we are victorious in Him. That was why Miss Williams told me earlier that I was wicked. All her little black tricks could not penetrate the undiluted Blood of Jesus Christ. We have to use the authority that Jesus Christ came into this world and gave us as His sons and daughters. Jesus Christ came to undo what Satan did in the Garden of Eden by shedding His Blood to pay for our sins. We are the ones who must learn not to bow to the god of this age. I am a living proof that you do not have to go "look" anywhere or rub up with all kind of ungodly scents, burn all different color candles and whatever else. If I were mixing Jesus Christ with evil many people would have taken me out a long time ago. The stronger one will always win because Satan does not care who dies as long as someone is killed or destroyed. Remember his mission is to rob, kill, steal and destroy according to John 10:10a. He is the Father of lies so he will make you feel powerful in the beginning but know that payday is coming. He does not give anything for free.

There was a lady who had a business in the building that I work in. She was always trying to guess people's birthday and their blood type. She claimed that God was giving her this information about others. She came to me one day and her information was wrong. I told her that she was dabbling in divination and with familiar spirits and it was not of God. She claimed to be a Christian so I warned her about opening these doors. She had a strong religious spirit so I informed her not to try and use me as a practice tool.

She came to me another day with a list in her hand of names of people that she claimed God told her to warn. I was at the top of her list. She said that God told her that I was aggressive. I asked her if I had ever been aggressive toward her and she said no. However, she claimed that God gave her the message. I thanked her for the information and then, of course, I examined myself.

Two days after this encounter Bishop T.D. Jakes was in Washington DC at the Convention Center. In his message one of his reference scriptures was Joshua 5:13-15 when the captain of the host visited Joshua. Bishop Jakes said and I am paraphrasing, that some of you have a strong warrior spirit and folks will want to criticize you but that is the Enemy's desire to get you to be lackadaisical in the things of God. He says let them continue to criticize you. I was so grateful to God for confirming what was in my spirit. Sometime when the word of God hits my spirit I tend to jump a lot on the spot. I jumped that night because my spirit was crying out "Yes Lord!" What a confirmation that was within the same week. When they cannot overpower you they criticize the anointing of God upon your life. What is so unfortunate is that some Christians become cold in their Christian walk as a result of criticism like this. They allow the fire of God to die because they so want to be liked by men.

This lady kept dabbling, opening ungodly spiritual doors and inviting strange people to come into the office at nights to pray with her. During this time she was very cold towards me. She rarely spoke to me unless it was absolutely necessary, which was fine because we did not work together. Every time I was on an extended fast it was as if she knew and was sent by the Enemy to disturb my spirit. She would say things that would at times be so hurtful. She was so spiritually twisted that she tried to convince me, by using scriptures, that God tells lies. I thank God that I am spiritually grounded because those religious spirits in her had to back down. Even though they did back down I knew that she really had a problem with me after that conversation. She would come over and greet others standing next to me and ignore me.

This went on for over a year until one day she was ready to speak. She said "Sister", now I became her sister, "Strange things are happening at nights when I am in the building alone". She went on to say that the lights over her side of the building would be turning on and off and she was not the one doing it. She said she has accessories that are brand new and when her customers come in to make a purchase they would not work. However, they would work after the customer was gone. I could tell that there was a lot more going on because of the fear that had gripped her. I encouraged her to continue praying.

The situation got even worse. She came back to me and said that strange things were happening at her home as well. She said that she could not sleep at night. She said she could hear sounds in her home as if other people were there with her. Things, her exact words, were being moved around in her house. Due to the fact that she could not sleep at night she became so tired that she felt as if she was losing her mind. She said, "Sis, could you come to my house and pray the demons out for me?" I respectfully declined.

On one occasion while asking me to come by her home she was very angry that her biological sister told her that the demons were not outside but that they were within her. If God is not sending me on an assignment I am not going. She eventually was forced to move and also to close her business. The last time I saw her she had moved to several homes and was having the same problem.

Even if you do not go to the witchcraft worker the Lord wants you to walk circumspectly because the days are evil. You have to be very careful with whom you connect in the spirit realm to pray in agreement. This lady opened several doors and she craved power and the gifts more than the Giver of the gifts. Some people only want power and the Enemy knows this so he tricks them. In Acts chapter 8 Simon the Sorcerer was impressed with the power of the Holy Spirit and thought that he could purchase it. Peter strongly rebuked him because his heart was not right.

If you believe that there is nothing wrong in mixing Jesus Christ with any other medium then my brothers and sisters your heart is also not right. The Lord is encouraging you to repent and turn from evil.

I believe that if you have ever had a deep revelation of the awesomeness of God Almighty you would never seek help outside of Him. In II Kings 6 there is an account of the Syrian army who was always planning strategies as to how to ambush the Israelite army. Every time the Syrian king plot his route, Elisha the prophet would inform the king of Israel which way not to travel otherwise they would be walking into a trap. The Syrian king got angry and very suspicious because he said there must be a traitor among his men giving information to the king of Israel. One of his men told him that was not the case but that there was a prophet in Israel who was able to tell the king of Israel everything that he (the Syrian king) spoke in his bedchamber.

The king of Syria was able to locate where Elisha was staying and so he had his army to surround the city of Dothan where he was. Early one morning when Elisha's servant came out he saw that the Syrian army had surrounded them with horses and chariots and he was very afraid. Elisha prayed to the Lord to open his eyes so that he may see that they that are with them are more than they that are against them. When the Lord opened the servant's eyes he saw that the mountain was surrounded with horses and chariots of fire, not just chariots but chariots of fire round about Elisha. Who can compete with our God?

COURAGE UNDER FIRE!!

God protects His people. He has not changed He is the same God yesterday, today and forever. What He did for Elisha and others in the scriptures He is well able to do for you and I today. That is why He is Almighty God, the Everlasting Father Who has taught His children to do battle but we have to adhere to His principles. He will not compete with any other god. Isaiah 43:10-11 says "Ye are my witnesses, saith the LORD, and my servant whom I have chosen: that ye may know and believe me, and understand that I am he: before me there was no God formed, neither shall there be after me. I, even I, am the Lord; and beside me there is no saviour."

On Monday, December 31, 2012 at about 12:30 am I sat at my computer editing Glen's testimony about his motorcycle accident. God heard my cry for my brother's soul and He was about to step in one more time. At 4:27 am that very morning the Enemy came into his home to finish the job but the Lord intervened again. He had an intense spiritual attack and witnessed the awesome power of the Blood of Jesus against the force of evil. The hand of God delivered him in such a mighty way that the experience shook him to the core of his being. The entire scene was being played out right before his eyes while he was wide awake. It is his testimony so I leave him to share it when the time is right.

David said in Psalm 40:1-2 "I waited patiently for the LORD; and he inclined unto me and heard my cry. He brought me up also out of an horrible pit, out of the miry clay, and set my feet upon a rock, and established my goings." I went to his home later that night and about 10:00 pm December 31, 2012 he surrendered his heart to the Lord. Only Jesus Christ saves and delivers so I will continue to trust Him for every need in my life. I am still striving but I have gained such deep trust for my Lord as a result of what I have experienced in my walk that I refuse to mix Jesus Christ.

If you are a Christian and you are faced with challenges and demonic attacks, then what you need to do is to go on a fast, read the word of God and worship Him. If you have committed any sin and or given the Enemy permission or legal right to come into your life then you need to close those doors by repenting of all sins. Find a Holy Ghost filled sister or brother if you are a male to pray with you but ask the Lord for direction. If you cannot handle the situation then seek help from your Pastor.

If you are not sure where you will spend eternity if you should die tonight, I encourage you to find a Bible believing church that is experienced in spiritual warfare so that they can pray for you to receive salvation and to be delivered.

You will save yourself and your family members a lot of heartache if you never mix Him. Satan's mission is not limited to only you. Oh no, he will come after you, your unborn child, your mother and your grandmother in a wheelchair. He does not care because he is that ruthless. If you trust Jesus Christ wholeheartedly you will have no regret because "He is able to do exceeding abundantly above all that we ask or think, according to the power that worketh in us." Ephesians 3:20.

Never mix Him!

COURAGE UNDER FIRE!!

THANKS

I hear the birds sing
I see the green leaves gently swaying in the wind
And I thank you Lord for dropping in.

You could have passed me by this morning
But your grace and mercy
Has blessed me with another precious day
Another day, Oh God, not to act foolish, confused or mean
But to show to the world what a joy
And wonder in my life you've been.

So this day I dare not take for granted
Cause I know too well the Savior's intent
A kind word or deed
A sincere prayer for a friend
Sharing God's divine plan to a lost or discouraged soul
Or a simple smile to let someone know I care.

With eyes closed, I listen to the birds sing
And whispered, thank you Lord for this morning.

Sheron M. Clarke
June 22, 1994

For speaking engagements Rev. Sheron M. Clarke of Ministry Without Walls International, Inc. may be contacted at (301) 642-8934 or via email clarke.sheron@yahoo.com.

You may also view the book dedication service of "Courage Under Fire" on Youtube at rev.sheronclarke@gmail.com.

www.ingramcontent.com/pod-product-compliance
Lightning Source LLC
LaVergne TN
LVHW051132080426
835510LV00018B/2360